WHAT ABOUT ME?

The Insider's Guide to Better Boundaries

STEPH STERNER

We are all responsible for the choices we make in our lives, regardless of where our ideas come from. It is always up to you what to say, how to say it and whether to say it at all. The purpose of this book is to help you to understand your options – and yourself – so that you can make better choices.

DEDICATION

This book is dedicated to everyone who has ever been afraid to say *no*. Whether you're being manipulated or abused, or you simply feel afraid, I hope that you find the courage to break free.

ACKNOWLEDGEMENTS

I'd like to thank everyone who has believed in me and supported me throughout my life. I am grateful for all the support I've received, especially from my parents and my amazing partner.
I couldn't do it without you!

WANT MORE … FOR FREE?

If you'd like to learn even more about boundaries – like how to recognize manipulation or how to use boundaries to improve your relationships – then head over to **stephsterner.com**. There are blog posts, quick tips and free downloads waiting for you.

And if you'd like something a bit more personal, you're invited to join Steph's private Facebook group: Boundaries and Bridges. You'll find it at **www.facebook.com/groups/boundariesandbridges/**. Ask questions, share your challenges and insight, get support when you need it … it's good to know you're not alone!

ALSO BY STEPH

No Guilt. No Games. No Drama
The 7 Keys to Setting Smarter Boundaries

If you're not sure when to set a boundary and when to go along, this book will get you on the right track.

Previous title:
Set Your Boundaries Your Way: No Guilt. No Games. No Drama

7 Easy Ways to Say NO to Almost Anyone:
Stand Up for Yourself Without Looking (or Feeling)
Unreasonable, Uncaring or Unkind

Cat got your tongue? No problem! This book will show you how to say *no* to all kinds of people. With plenty of options for all kinds of situations, you're sure to find something that works for you.

All of Steph's books are available on **amazon.com** – and of course you can find everything on **stephsterner.com**.

TABLE OF CONTENTS

4TH CHAPTER: ARE YOUR EMOTIONS RUNNING THE SHOW?   65

5TH CHAPTER: LOOKING FOR APPROVAL?   79

6ᵀᴴ CHAPTER: STUCK IN THE GUILT TRAP?   95

7ᵀᴴ CHAPTER: WHO'S PRESSURING YOU?   109

PREFACE

WHAT THIS BOOK
CAN DO FOR YOU

D o you ever wonder what happened to your life? Does it feel like you're in a movie, reading the lines you've been given? Or maybe you've been writing your own lines, but it's just not working out. Other people seem to be getting what they want from their lives – so why not you?

It's easy to lose yourself these days. There's family, friends, work … even the internet can steal your time and energy. And before you know it, it feels like you're simply existing. The enjoyment, the sense of purpose … they slipped away when you weren't looking.

If it's the internet that's taken over your life, you could try a digital detox. But what if it's people? You can't just run off to a desert island – or tell your boss, your friends and your family that they'll have to wait until you've figured out what's wrong with your life. If you're losing yourself in others, spending too much of your life focused on their needs, you can't just go cold turkey.

So what **can** you do?

If your life is not your own, chances are you've given it away a piece at a time, in a hundred different ways. No single decision made your life feel empty or meaningless. If you want to get your life back, you'll need to make better choices. That means setting some boundaries – and that may make you uncomfortable.

Don't worry; you're not alone. Standing up for yourself can lead to conflict and rejection. It can make you feel guilty for putting yourself first. And if you're dealing with someone who gets aggressive, it can be downright scary.

It can be tempting to think that the problem lies with the people around you. Why do they expect so much of you? Why don't they take some responsibility for a change? But then you realize that other people aren't having this problem – even though they spend time with those same people. So it must be you. You may start to wonder: "What's wrong with me?"

Let me put an end to these worries right now. There's nothing wrong with you. The qualities that can make you a pushover are the same ones that make you a kind, caring, generous person.

Is that it? Do you have to choose between being a good person and having a life of your own?

Absolutely not!

You **can** have both. You **can** care about others and still have a life. But it takes some work. I know because I've been there.

I've learned that there are many ways to give your life away. I've also learned that we're not even aware of most of them – which makes change a bit difficult. Here are just some of the ways we sabotage ourselves:

- We agree to things we don't have time for.
- We go along with things that don't feel right.
- We don't know what we **really** want.
- We don't ask for what we want.
- When we do ask for what we want, people don't fully understand us.
- We treat the things that matter most as favors, asking for them but never insisting.
- When we do set boundaries, our discomfort shows in our body language.

- We live our lives according to someone else's rules (parents, spouses, cultures, religions, etc.).
- We do what we're supposed to do rather than what feels right.
- We expect others know what our boundaries are.
- We expect others to honor our boundaries once we've expressed them.
- We put others first, even when our needs matter more.
- We make excuses for bad behavior.
- We don't hold people accountable – which means they never learn.
- We assume that what others want must be important. Why else would they be pushing so hard?
- We keep the peace at all costs.
- We forgive and forget – when we should be learning.
- We assume the best of others, even when they show us their worst.
- We look after everyone but ourselves.
- We create "boundaries" with no consequences, so honoring them is optional.
- We give in at the first sign of resistance.
- We let our emotions run the show.

Clearly we have too many ways to stop ourselves. So where do you start?

Right here, with this book. Each chapter delivers a different piece of the puzzle. You may not need them all, but it's important to know what they are. Because until then, you won't know what questions to ask.

You see, the key to solving any problem lies in asking the right questions. If you're too focused on others to have time for yourself, why is that? Do you see yourself as the great fixer, the one everyone can depend on to make things right? Do you agree to things that don't work for you because you can't say *no*? Or do you worry that if you don't take care of things, no one will?

This is just the beginning of the questions you'll need to ask yourself. If you can't say *no*, what stops you? If you need to be the dependable one, why is that? And what's your definition of *dependable*?

The purpose of this book is to help you find both the questions and the answers. Here are just some of the things you'll learn:

- 8 reasons you don't trust your instincts;
- 17 half-truths that stop you from living your own life;
- 8 communication mistakes that destroy your boundaries;
- 8 ways your emotions can hijack your decisions, sometimes without you even knowing it;
- Why people-pleasing is often a form of manipulation – and why it can never give you what you truly want;
- 7 guilt traps and how to escape them;
- 4 types of pressure and how to overcome them gracefully; and
- 8 clues that you might be paying more attention to other people's opinions than your own.

And finally, we'll cover how to tell when you don't need a boundary at all – even though it feels like you do.

I've been there, and I know how hard change can be. I also know how liberating it is to finally draw the line. So keep reading. Learn about yourself, learn about setting boundaries – and then start doing it. Your life will never be the same.

INTRODUCTION

WHAT IS A BOUNDARY, ANYWAY?

E veryone likes Kyra. She's thoughtful, reliable and generous to a fault. If you find yourself in a tough spot, Kyra will save the day. And she doesn't expect anything in return. Kyra is all about service; she can't imagine a life without it.

But lately she's been feeling more resentful than helpful. She's noticed that people expect her to drop what she's doing to help them; they don't ask the way they used to. And they no longer seem to appreciate the sacrifices she makes for them. She used to get flowers and thank-you notes. Now she gets taken for granted.

Kyra realized that, whether it seemed selfish or not, she needed some time for her own priorities. She decided to start her day with affirmations and beautiful music before going through her to-do list. She asked her friends and relatives not to call her until lunch time; that way she could focus on her own needs before helping others. She was so excited about her new schedule. Once she got that to-do list under control, she'd have time for some creative projects. And she'd be able to support her friends and family without resenting them.

The first few days were blissful. But then the morning phone calls started again. The conversation was always the same:

"I know I'm not supposed to call before lunch, but I didn't know where else to turn...."

I'm trying to get some things done. Can't it wait?

"I wish it could, but it can't. If I don't deal with this right now ..."

OK (sighing). *What do you need?*

When Kyra set her boundary, she thought things would get better. Everyone would understand that she needed some time to herself, and she'd finally get some balance in her life. She could have it all: time for herself and time for everyone else. But it didn't work out that way. It seemed people depended on her too much to get along without her, even for the morning. Kyra felt more miserable than ever.

Joe is a "regular guy." He's honest, trustworthy and hard-working. He has a few friends at work, and a few more at church. Although he'd like more, he's grateful for the ones he has. Last year he had the chance to become a supervisor, but he refused. He said he just wouldn't feel right being in charge; he'd rather be part of the team.

Recently Mark, an easy-going guy a few years younger than Joe, joined his group. They both liked the same teams, so there was always plenty to talk about after a game. When Mark invited him to join his Friday night poker game, Joe felt like he was back in high school and finally part of the "in" crowd.

A month or two later, Mark started coming back late from lunch. Often. And he had trouble focusing on his work (especially around attractive women). Joe had to pick up the slack; they were on a tight deadline, and his boss would not be happy if their work wasn't up to speed.

One day the boss asked Joe to stop by his office on his way in the next morning. He wanted to know how the new guy was working out.

Joe couldn't sleep that night. He didn't like being taken advantage of by Mark, but he didn't want to give up Friday nights with the guys. He'd always felt like an outsider, and he finally fit in. He didn't want to lie to the boss, but he didn't want to lose his newfound sense of belonging, either. When the alarm finally went off, Joe still didn't know what to do.

Laura was always the pretty one. When she turned 30, she decided her looks wouldn't last forever, so she started going for expensive beauty treatments. Her friends told her she was crazy, but her response was always the same: "Better safe than sorry."

She could have almost any man she wanted, but she always picked the wrong ones. They would wine and dine her, tell her how beautiful and caring she was – nothing like those other women they'd been with – and before long, they'd be moving in. And then they'd change before her very eyes. Suddenly her clothes were too revealing, her hair was all wrong and she was the most selfish partner in the world. She'd try her best to make it work, doing whatever they wanted, but it was never enough. Laura couldn't bring herself to give up on these men, but eventually they would leave her for someone younger, prettier or more accommodating. And she was left wondering what would have happened if she'd tried a little harder.

"This time will be different," she would tell herself. "This time I'm going to get it right."

What these three have in common is their unwillingness to set (or, in Kyra's case, maintain) healthy boundaries. They allow others to take advantage of them in some way, and they don't feel good when they do.

The True Nature of Boundaries

The first mistake we make with respect to boundaries is to misunderstand their nature. A boundary begins with what you will and will not tolerate in your life. It says, "this far and no farther." But that's only half the story. "My sister mustn't expect to use my vacation home every month when she never even calls to ask how I'm doing," is not a boundary. This is a boundary:

I won't allow people who don't show any interest in me to use my vacation home. That includes my sister.

Please understand something: I'm not suggesting that this is a good boundary (or a bad one, either). If you feel hurt by someone in your family, I hope you'll try to heal your relationship. If you've passed that point, then only you can decide where your boundaries lie. Just remember that "She mustn't ..." doesn't define a boundary. Boundary statements begin with phrases like "I will" or "I won't." That's because your boundaries are about you, your values and the choices you make. When someone violates those values, you must decide what to do about it. That's the other half of the boundary: your response.

Crossing That Line

Boundaries are lines that you don't want someone to cross. When others don't respect these lines, it's up to you to change their minds. How you do that depends on you and your relationships. Sometimes we're not sure what to do. And sometimes we know what needs to be done, but we can't bring ourselves to do it. If you're in either of these situations, this book is for you.

The purpose of this book is to explore the many ways we give away our power – and how to take it back gracefully. It will help you to see where, how and why you're sabotaging yourself. After all, you can't fix things until you understand where they're broken.

Often when we give away our power, it's because we don't have enough confidence in ourselves. Many of us trust other people's opinions (and judgments) more than our own. Keep reading to learn the eight reasons we don't trust our instincts, why it's important to question where your beliefs come from – and who they serve – and what to do when even the truth can't set you free.

1ST CHAPTER

DO YOU TRUST YOURSELF?

When Maureen and her friends arrive, the party is in full swing. It's Friday night, and everyone is celebrating. Except Maureen. She glances around nervously, searching for the source of her discomfort. But everything looks fine. When she mentions her feelings to one of her friends, she laughs and tells her she's been working too hard. "Have a drink and get over yourself," she says. Maureen feels silly, worrying about nothing … but the feeling won't go away.

She stays, but she never relaxes. She sips some wine, but that makes her stomach feel worse. She wishes she were home watching TV, but she tells herself she's being ridiculous. She needs to lighten up.

Just after midnight, when she's finally started to relax and dance a bit, the police storm in. Three or four party-goers are arrested for possession, and another is accused of dealing. Everyone is taken to the police station for questioning. Maureen spends a long night worrying about going to jail for showing up at the wrong party. After much questioning, she and her friends are finally released.

Not Trusting Your Gut

How often have you used logic to discount your intuition and avoid setting a boundary? How foolish did you feel when you realized that your gut feeling was right? Have you ever wondered **why** you don't trust that sixth sense?

According to one definition, intuition is "perception via the unconscious". The Western mind mistrusts the unconscious because it can never be understood. And we **must** understand! To reach this understanding, we rely on three things:

- information (or, more accurately, subjective interpretations of information);
- beliefs (which are simply subjective interpretations of experience); and
- logic (which must be based on information and beliefs).

These elements form the basis of objective understanding. Anything else comes from the dark realm of the unconscious. And let's face it: we're afraid of the dark.

What makes intuition so valuable is that it gives us a glimpse into our own unconscious. Unfortunately, it's often no more than that. In *Blink: The Power of Thinking Without Thinking*, Malcolm Gladwell describes it this way:

> *Insight is not a light bulb that goes off*
> *inside our heads. It is a flickering candle*
> *that can easily be snuffed out.*

Without this insight, we are limited to what we can consciously understand. We ignore the clues picked up by the unconscious and stay within the comfort zone of our information, beliefs and logic. Sometimes that works, but sometimes we miss what's most important. As Abelia Arthur put it, intuition allows us to "cut through the thickness of surface reality". And when things are not as they seem, that's exactly what we need.

Trusting your gut doesn't mean acting as if every little twinge is significant – or correct. It means taking that unsettled feeling (or that totally irrational excitement) into account. In Maureen's case, that could have translated into giving up a party that she wasn't enjoying in exchange for her peace of mind – and a good night's sleep.

On a more mundane level, this can mean asking questions before agreeing to something. You may discover something unexpected that explains your concern – or you may realize that everything's alright after all. But you won't know how to respond until you get more information. When you do that, you turn that "flickering candle" into a steady flame. And then it's not so dark.

Trusting Others More than Yourself

Some people exude confidence. They speak with authority, even when they don't know what they're talking about. Whether their opinions have been carefully considered or chosen in the heat of the moment, they sound good. Their certainty makes you wonder how you could ever question them.

And some people are just the opposite. They trust other people's judgment more than their own. The opinions behind their decisions come from someone else, so they're based on someone else's values and life experience. These people only make good decisions when the people they consult with have similar values and beliefs – and no conflicting agendas.

Plenty of people are willing to tell us how to look after a baby, how to spend our money, how much to put up with from the boss … the list goes on. But no amount of advice can ever solve the real problem. If you don't know and trust yourself, you simply won't make good decisions – at least, not consistently.

Steve just graduated from college, and he has three job offers. He's pretty sure he can eliminate one, but he doesn't know how to choose between the other two. His friends and family all have opinions. His father says that the higher-paying job is the best. In a few years, he'll be ready to move on; employers will look at his current salary before making an offer. "You're young," he says. "This is the best approach when you're young."

Although he's still unsure, Steve decides that his father makes sense. He's a successful businessman, so his advice should be the best. Then he runs into an old friend, someone he hasn't seen in a few years. They meet for lunch and he shares his dilemma. His friend asks him some interesting questions – questions Steve has never considered.

"What's the best thing about each position?" he asks. "What's the worst?" He continues, "What do you think of the companies and the people you've met? And what about the work? Will it be challenging? Will you enjoy it? You don't want to spend all day doing something you don't like just because it pays more."

As he and his friend spoke, Steve began to understand his options. He realized that the lower-paying job was better for him. He would enjoy it more, and it would prepare him for the work he wanted to do later. Steve had never asked himself the most important question: *What do I want?* Because his friend encouraged him to consider it from many perspectives, he could see what was best for him.

Steve's only concern was how to tell his father. When asked why he settled for less money, Steve explained his reasons. His father beamed. "Son, I suggested the other job because you weren't sure of yourself. And when all else is equal, it's best to take the higher salary. But I can see that you've thought about this carefully and you know what you want. You're making a good decision."

Steve was grateful for his father's support, but he also knew that his decision stood on its own. At the end of the day, you're the ultimate authority on what's best for you. If you have friends who are "experts," I hope that their expertise lies in asking you the right questions. When it comes to important decisions, that's often the only help you need.

Not Knowing Yourself Well Enough

Getting to know yourself is one of the most important things you can do in this life. People who don't know themselves well often struggle. Many find themselves on an emotional roller coaster, with their buttons constantly being pushed. They tend to have a tough time making decisions, as they don't know what's most important to them.

Being clear about your values simplifies just about any decision. If you know that you value honesty more than anything else, then you will never agree to a "little white lie." You won't tolerate dishonest business practices, and you'll refuse to associate with people who distort the truth to manipulate you. When someone asks (or expects) you to lie for them, you'll simply refuse. You may also find yourself wondering how many "little white lies" this person has told you!

If keeping the peace is more important to you, you may be prepared to misrepresent the truth to avoid an unnecessary conflict – particularly if you believe that the truth involved is not a terribly important one. (For example, if were asked to repeat a potentially hurtful remark, you might change the wording a bit to remove the sting.) If keeping commitments is high on your list, then you won't have much time for people who break theirs. Knowing what matters most to you makes it easier to decide when to set a boundary and when to simply "go with the flow".

It's also important to know your emotional buttons. If you get aggressive when people keep you waiting, you might decide to keep quiet when it happens rather than explode and feel guilty or embarrassed afterwards. You might also decide how long you're willing to wait for certain people. Letting them know how long you'll wait – and leaving if they don't arrive in time – is one way to ensure that your time is respected.

If you're afraid of conflict and tend to give in rather than get into a fight, others can easily use this to manipulate you. Knowing this about yourself, you might take yourself out of the situation so you can think clearly. If you need to give an answer, and it's not the one someone's looking for, try to avoid doing it in person. A phone call may be less intimidating, and you'll find it easier to end the conversation. (An email or text is even easier, if it's appropriate.)

Once you know your buttons, you can start finding ways to work around them.

If you need to tiptoe around your fears too often, I encourage you to get some help with your emotions. Then you'll be free to set the boundaries that matter to you, regardless of what others say or do. When you heal your wounds, no one can use them against you.

When the Truth Doesn't Set You Free

A teenager sees her father with another woman. He gets flustered and quickly explains that they work together and she brought him something he needed from the office. But the way the woman is dressed, the way they looked at each other – she knows something is wrong. If she's right, then her father is a liar and a cheat. She'd rather be wrong. It all seems simple enough, except for one "small" problem: She's learned not to trust her instincts.

One divorce and one teenage son later, Rosemary meets a man who seems too good to be true. He compliments her regularly, buys her gifts and even laughs at her jokes. (Even her closest friends don't do that!) When he proposes, Rosemary is in heaven. The wedding is beautiful, and it seems that life can't get any better.

A year and a half later, Rosemary is pregnant with her second child. She's getting ready to resign from her job to be a full-time mom, something she'd never thought possible. But she's not happy. Just when she should be on top of the world, she feels terribly insecure. When her friends and family ask what's wrong, she says, "I feel as if the other shoe is about to drop. Isn't that crazy?" They all agree that she is, in fact, crazy – but pregnancy can do that to a woman. She'll be fine once the baby is born.

Then one day the unthinkable happens. One of her old friends, whom she hasn't seen since the wedding, calls her unexpectedly. Rosemary is thrilled to hear her voice – until she learns the reason for her call.

"I'm sorry to have to tell you this, but you need to know. I saw your husband at lunch with a woman today. At first, I thought it was just a business lunch. But as I turned to get up from the table, I saw him give her something. I couldn't see what it was, but it was in a beautiful, gift-wrapped box. I'm sorry, honey, but it looks like he's cheating on you."

Rosemary thanks her friend and hangs up the phone in shock. She realizes that she's not crazy at all. The mysterious phone calls, the late nights at the office – it all makes sense. Still … it **can't** be true. There must be another explanation – for the late nights, the changes in their relationship…. She wracks her brain for ideas, but nothing comes.

Rosemary suffers from a terrible inner conflict: *I know, but I can't know.* She can't face the truth because she's afraid of what it means to her:

- *I was wrong about him all along.*
- *He's a liar and a cheat, just like my father.*
- *He never loved me.*
- *I'm a fool.*
- *I need to leave him, the sooner the better.*

She's not ready to face any of this, especially with another baby on the way, so she continues as if nothing is wrong. She knows there must be a good explanation, even though she can't imagine what that could be. And she decides not to insult him by asking.

If something doesn't feel right, it probably isn't.

That nagging feeling that something's wrong is an important signal. If something doesn't feel right, it probably isn't. Ask yourself some tough questions, and dig deep for the answers. The sooner you face a difficult situation, the sooner you can deal with it.

Following Someone Else's Rules

Most of us have a "code" that we live by, a set of rules that govern our behavior. We developed some of these rules over time, as we learned more about ourselves and the people around us. Others we created in an instant, to avoid emotional pain. The rest came from parents and other authority figures as well as society at large.

It's important to question these rules once in a while, to see whether they still work. For example, Joanne grew up with an alcoholic father and a mother who spent most her time trying to avoid his rage. Her mother gave her (primarily by example) some rules to live by:

- Keep everyone happy.
- Never stir up trouble.
- Always let the man be right.
- Fix everyone else's problems before they become your own.

When she was younger, it made sense to copy her mother's coping strategies; they seemed to keep her father under control. But what about today? Are they still useful? Let's see how they affect her life:

Keep everyone happy. Does Joanne really need to keep everyone happy all the time? Is that even possible? Let's look at the coming weekend. Her husband wants to unwind after a tough week at the office by playing golf on Saturday, which means he won't be available to drive the kids around. Her brother wants to bring his two-year-old over on Saturday morning so that he and his wife can have a few hours of peace and quiet. He says they'll pick him up before lunch, but they never do. The kids have invited their friends to go swimming on Sunday. Her husband watches sports on Sunday afternoons; this ritual has been in place since their first weekend of married life. On top of all that, there's an important deadline at work; Joanne's team is behind schedule. And she isn't ready for Monday's management presentation, as she's been busy helping the team catch up.

If Joanne gets up early on Sunday, she can still make some time for her presentation. But will it be enough? And what about her team? They expect her to be at the office on Saturday morning, while her husband plays golf and her brother uses her as a babysitter. And the in-laws haven't even called yet. They'll want Joanne to bring the kids over. But when?

Never stir up trouble. Maybe it's OK to stir things up now and then. After all, nothing ever changes unless someone resists the status quo. And that always stirs up something! When she was younger, "stirring things up" was dangerous for Joanne and her family. But maybe that's exactly what she needs to do now.

What would it mean to "stir things up"? For Joanne, it could be as simple as telling her brother that she'd like to alternate weekends with the kids so that she has some peace and quiet, too. It could also mean getting her husband more involved with the kids on the weekend. She's been doing all the work for years.

There are plenty of other ways that Joanne could get some free time. The good news is that she doesn't need to do them all, or do any of them all the time. But if she wants a few hours for herself, she'll have to make some changes.

Always let the man be right. Sometimes letting someone else be right means making yourself wrong. Joanne has allowed her husband to make all the decisions in their family. If he doesn't like what she's wearing, she changes her clothes. If he thinks that his taxes shouldn't be wasted on art and music, who is she to argue? And when he says he's earned the right to a weekly golf game, she's never once pointed out that she works harder than he does. She doesn't assert herself, even in small ways, because she's afraid of his response. After all these years, she's still afraid of her father's rage. This keeps her safe but unfulfilled. That empty feeling just won't go away.

Fix everyone else's problems before they become your own. This worked when Joanne was a child, but now she finds herself resenting her family, friends and co-workers. Trying to solve their problems takes away any time she might have to relax. She spends most evenings on the phone, giving advice. Her mother is always being treated unfairly by someone, and there's never anything she can do about it. Like her mother, the friends she has attracted prefer complaining to taking action. Everything is always someone else's fault, so their problems can never be solved. Being surrounded by negativity and the victim mentality keeps Joanne feeling helpless and hopeless.

It seems that Joanne's childhood strategies now carry a rather large price tag. Her life is not her own, and her time with friends and family leaves her tired and resentful. Following her mother's rules has given her a life like her mother's – the last thing she ever wanted.

Here are some other rules that many of us have inherited from our parents and other authority figures:

- Your job comes first.
- Your family comes first.
- Be loyal to your family and friends, even when they're wrong.
- You can't say *no* to you parents (or your spouse or your boss). It's disrespectful.
- When your husband is unhappy, it's up to you to cheer him up. You won't be happy until he is.

If any of these apply to you, I encourage you to think about the impact they have on your life right now. If your rules no longer work for you, replace them with better ones. Your happiness depends upon your ability to change.

Not Knowing What You Want

Boundaries are about what you want and what you don't want, what's OK with you and what isn't. We want many things:

- approval;
- respect;
- acknowledgement that we're right;
- status;
- a sense of belonging;
- time for the things that matter to us;
- favors;
- money or gifts;
- feeling important or needed; and
- other good feelings about ourselves and the choices we make.

And we often want to avoid things:

- disapproval;
- disrespect;
- rejection;
- conflict;
- guilt;
- embarrassment, shame or humiliation; and
- feelings of inferiority or low self-esteem.

Of course, we can't have it all. There are always trade-offs. To avoid conflict, we may need to let go of proving that we're right. To have time for the things that matter to us, we may need to manage without someone's approval – or even risk conflict and rejection.

Maureen isn't happy at work; she finds another job and resigns. The head of her department asks her to stay, offering her a raise. She doesn't know what to do. Why? Because she isn't clear about what she wants. If she resigned because she's bored, the extra money won't solve her problem. In that case, she might consider talking to the department head about taking on more or different responsibilities. Or she might take that new job, especially if it's more challenging or interesting than this one. But if she resigned because she wanted more money or didn't feel appreciated, she may want to reconsider.

Maureen may want a few things: more money, appreciation, interesting work or even a more positive environment. But until she figures out what she wants the most, she won't know what to do.

Thinking That What You Want Is Wrong

It's time for Sam to fill out his college applications. His father has suggested several good business schools. The knot in his stomach grows tighter with each form. Sam's real love is art; he spends most of his free time creating elaborate fantasy characters on his computer. Numbers don't interest him. He can't imagine how he'll ever learn to read a balance sheet or evaluate a potential investment – or why anyone would want to.

But Sam's father expects him to take over his medical supply business one day. He's a successful businessman, and he wants nothing less for his only son. Sam applies to business schools, secretly hoping he won't be accepted – and feeling guilty in the process. He's completed the application for a local graphic arts program, but he's still working up the nerve to send it in.

Sometimes we let others – especially authority figures and people close to us – decide what we "should" do. We take on their opinions or desires, even when they conflict with our own. We decide that what we want is wrong, or that we can't have it.

And so the conflict begins. Which voice do we obey?

One of those voices may belong to society at large rather than any individual. Society (as understood by you) may say that a woman of your intelligence must pursue a career. You can have children later, once you've established yourself. Your society may say that a young person should find a good job; starting your own business is too risky. Or it may say that all politicians are owned by their supporters, and an honest one will never get elected.

Ask yourself what you really believe –
and what you really want.

It's important to see these voices for what they are: other people's opinions. Question them. Ask yourself what you really believe – and what you really want. Do you want to focus on your career first, or is it more important to you to start a family? Do you want to start your own business? What are you willing to sacrifice to make it succeed? Is politics where your heart lies? If so, how will you deal with the challenges? What would your first steps be?

It isn't always a parent telling you to give up your dream. Sometimes it's no one in particular – just a belief you picked up along the way or a lack of confidence in yourself. Don't let fear, guilt or self-doubt destroy your dreams. Convincing yourself that someone else knows better, or that you're wrong for wanting something like a family or a business, is painful. It's also a recipe for failure. If you want something, let yourself want it. Then find a way to get it.

Ignoring Inner Conflicts

"I've figured out how to get that job – you know, the one at the magazine."

But don't they want someone with experience?

"They do. That's where you come in ..."

Kyra feels that familiar churning in her stomach as Jenny's words sink in. Her throat goes dry as she forces the words out:

Where I come in? What do I have to do with you getting a job?

Of course, Kyra already knows the answer: Jenny expects her to lie for her. She's probably already doctored her resumé to include a stint at Kyra's company.

Having confirmed the details, Jenny senses her hesitation.

"Come on ... you owe me. How am I ever supposed to get a job if everyone wants someone with experience? And besides, it's no big deal. I just need you to give them a good reason to interview me. The rest is up to me."

Kyra was speechless. No one had stood by her like Jenny. But what she was asking …

Jenny is telling her that this is what friends do for each other. But real friends don't pressure you into violating your values. And they don't treat your relationship like a series of transactions.

Kyra has two conflicting desires: to keep Jenny happy and to feel good about herself. Doing this favor will cost her dearly, and she knows it. She needs to face this conflict head-on and decide what's most important to her. Looking at the kind of relationships she wants in her life might be a good place to start.

This example is rather blatant. Most of us would agree that Jenny is being unreasonable and Kyra's conflict is a sign that she's not secure in herself. But the principle applies even when it's less obvious. If you don't like to lie, then even a little bit of dishonesty will create an inner conflict. So will treating someone unfairly, taking advantage of someone else's mistake, or anything else that violates your values.

That uncomfortable feeling is a warning sign. It's telling you to resolve the conflict before you agree to anything. You would be wise to listen.

It Takes Courage

Knowing and trusting ourselves is the foundation for good decisions – and the strength to implement them. If you realize that others are leading your life, or if you suspect that you're avoiding a painful truth, I hope you'll find the courage to face this challenge head-on. You may need help from family, friends or professionals. That's OK. We don't need to do everything ourselves. Get the support you need and take those first brave steps toward living your own life. There's nothing like it!

Of course, some of us already trust ourselves – at least enough to get by. The obstacles we face are less obvious. You may be surprised to learn that there are at least 17 half-truths – which too many of us believe – that stop us from doing what's right for us. Keep reading to learn which ones you believe and how they're affecting your life.

2ND CHAPTER

DO   WHAT DO YOU BELIEVE?

B eliefs and expectations can be a huge source of boundary issues. Without even thinking about it, you expect those close to you to follow certain rules. Everyone's rules are slightly different, and we each have our own hierarchy. We may assume the following about our family and friends:

- They'll never lie to us.
- They'll respect our privacy.
- They'll never embarrass us.
- They'll give us emotional support when we need it.
- They'll give us space when we need it.
- They won't try to force their values on us.
- They'll love and accept us as we are.

These are just some of the things we may take for granted. And based on our history, we may have very specific expectations of each of our loved ones. Often we're not even aware of what they are.

But very few people will always live up to our expectations. And when they don't, we feel blindsided. We react with shock and pain: "How could she?" or "Why didn't I see this coming? I thought I knew him!" Anyone surprised by a spouse's infidelity understands how hard this can be.

It pays to make our beliefs and expectations conscious – and to question them every so often. I'm not suggesting that this will spare us the pain of betrayal. But it will certainly help us to become more realistic. It will also get us thinking about how to respond when people ignore our wants and needs. Let's look at the rather long list of false beliefs and unrealistic expectations – those beautiful lies – that stand in the way of setting healthy boundaries.

Others Share Your Values

At our core, we're very much the same. We want to be loved. We want to feel special. We want to be told the truth.

And although most of us seem to share the same basic values, we each apply them in our own way. Some people think it's OK to sacrifice honesty for kindness (or even money); others will tell the truth no matter what the cost. Some look for respect and acknowledgement in their work; others just want their salary and benefits. Some trust strangers and assume the best of everyone, while others are waiting for the first sign of trouble.

It's probably safe to say that we all value honesty and respect in others. After all, we all want to hear the truth (at least most of the time!) and to be treated well. But to assume that those around us will consistently place these values above all others is unrealistic. The people whom you know well may behave predictably. Your sister who values kindness and trust over honesty may "forget" to tell you a few things because they're hurtful. But she won't skip anything important; that would violate your trust. Your friend who is so concerned with appearances will consistently present himself in the most flattering light possible – and you know that he won't make anyone look bad in the process. But your new boss may be a mystery.

We tend to think we know people well until they do something that violates our values. Then we conclude that we never knew them at all.

We often think we know people better than we do. You may resent your mother's sudden interest in your personal life. That "really nice guy" at the office may keep leaving his paperwork on your desk ("You're so good at this kind of thing...."). A friend may surprise you by asking for money repeatedly, even after you've made it clear that you're not willing to lend it. We tend to think we know people well until they do something that violates our values. Then we conclude that we never knew them at all. That's because, once we know they share some of our highest values, we think they share them all. This is seldom the case.

Occasionally people mislead us from the very beginning. A colleague of mine experienced this years ago. A woman decided that he was a good catch, and she was willing to use whatever bait was needed. She lied about her interests, talents and education – and who knows what else. She seemed perfect for him, so he ended the relationship he was in and they began dating. They were together for more than a year and even had a child.

Eventually he began to question the "common interests" that had so attracted him to her. She had a passion for music (and a degree from a top music school to go with it). She played several instruments. Or did she? Whenever he asked her to play, she wasn't in the right mood. He, on the other hand, loved music; he was always in the mood for it.

Needless to say, my colleague had been conned. The mother of his child had no musical talent. She had lied about her interests and her education to get her man.

Most situations are less dramatic, but we still feel the shock:

- *I expected more of him.*

- *I thought I could count on her.*
- *I guess people change....*

These situations remind us that our understanding of the other was incomplete, as it must be. We can never fully know another human being. Life and relationships are full of risks. Being realistic about others can help us to accept these risks and respond to them gracefully.

People Will Respect Your Boundaries Once You Express Them

It makes sense that, except with those who know you well, you need to express your boundaries clearly before they'll be respected. If you don't say *no*, someone will assume a *yes*. Some people struggle to put their boundaries into words. It feels rude somehow, as if it shouldn't be necessary. And what if there's an argument?

It seems only fair that, once you get past these obstacles, your problems should be over. But that's not always the case. Some people simply will not respect your boundaries – at least, not when they want something from you. (Remember how Kyra's friends responded when she asked them not to call in the morning.) They tend to give lip service to your rights:

- "Of course, I completely understand your need for privacy."
- "I can see how busy you are ..."
- "I know I promised I wouldn't ask you to do this, but ..."

They acknowledge your boundary and then do their best to walk all over it. That's because acknowledging it softens the blow. It makes them look like kind and caring people who really need you – rather than selfish individuals who aren't interested in you at all. Of course, the truth usually lies somewhere between those two extremes.

What happens when you tell that nice man who leaves his paperwork on your desk that you have your own deadlines to meet? If he's a "lip service guy", he'll use any tactic he can to change your mind:

"I know you do, and you know I wouldn't ask if it wasn't so important. My boss is really after me for this, and I'm miserable at it. I don't know what I'd do without you!" or

"I know you're busy, too. It would mean so much to me, though. I owe you big time!" – spoken as he hurries off to lunch with his buddies.

Under these circumstances, your job is to take a deep breath, return his paperwork, and let him know you won't be doing it for him. No further explanation needed.

People will only respect your boundaries when it suits them. When it doesn't, they won't. Don't assume everyone is respectful. Be prepared to stand up to those who aren't. They'll eventually learn that disrespecting you doesn't pay.

People Who Care Will Always Respect Your Boundaries

We tend to assume that the people we're close to will take our feelings into account. They know what matters to us, and they would never hurt us. But this isn't completely true. Let's look at each part of this assumption separately.

The people closest to you know how you feel. This is often true. By now, everyone in your family knows you're sensitive about your premature gray. No one jokes about it, because they know you won't be laughing. But not everyone understands how much you value your privacy – or what you consider to be private. So when your brother-in-law asks you how much money came with that big promotion, you don't need to storm off in a huff. Just let him know where your boundary is. "I don't talk about my finances. But I will say I'm very happy with my new job … and my new salary." Now he knows you don't share the dollars and cents (or whatever your currency is), and no one needs to feel uncomfortable.

Most people, rather than picking up on subtle cues, take it for granted that our boundaries are like theirs. Someone who's comfortable with friends dropping by unannounced may assume the same of you. Unless you've told others how important an issue is to you (or shown them through your actions), don't assume they know. Tell them. (Women, this can be especially true of men. If your husband says or does something that you find hurtful, stop making him guess what's wrong! Talk to him about how you feel. Until he understands, he'll keep doing it.)

They would never hurt you. There are people who would never do anything to hurt the ones they love; nothing matters more to them. But with everyone else, there's always the chance they might trample over your boundaries under the "right" circumstances. Sometimes people don't respect a boundary because they don't believe you're entitled to it. Sometimes they're angry and ignore your wishes just to get back at you. But usually something matters more to them than respecting you. Often that "something" is not so obvious.

Peter and Diane have chosen Friday night as date night. It's the one time in the week they can get away from the kids and spend some quality time together. But Diane's mother, who's "never heard of such nonsense", schedules family events on Friday evenings and expects them to be there. "Have your 'date' on Saturday night – or wait until next week. Stop being so selfish!"

Can you hear the resentment? Her own husband never set aside time to be with her ... and he probably never will. Peter's devotedness **hurts**. It reminds her of what's missing in her own marriage. Before "date night" she could tell herself that men don't appreciate their wives. Now she must face the fact that some of them do. Without even realizing it, she's trying to make her pain go away by removing the trigger. Date night reminds her that she's jealous of her own daughter's happiness.

When faced with a choice between giving in to their fears and respecting your boundaries, most people don't even realize they're making one. And those who do may still rationalize you right out of the picture:

- "You don't really need that money. You always say you don't have enough, but you're fine."

- "I knew you'd understand. After all, we're family."
- Or my personal favorite: "What **choice** did I have???"

When people you care about refuse to respect
your boundaries, it's up to you to enforce them.

It's important to realize that the people who care about you care even more about themselves. This is true for everyone. When our needs conflict with the needs of others, we all act from our own self-interest. That's human nature.

Our values and the emotional intensity of our needs and desires shape our responses. That's why some of us will put others first: our values dictate it. And that's why we're so shocked when others don't. We've misinterpreted their values or underestimated their emotional intensity. Fear and greed are powerful motivators.

When people you care about refuse to respect your boundaries, it's up to you to enforce them. Why would you lend money to someone who won't pay it back? Ask yourself this important question before making your decision. Consider walking away from people who become rude when they don't get their way. And refuse to engage in the same debate over and over. Your decision is your decision. You don't need to justify it to anyone.

Their Needs Are More Important

Many of us have been taught from an early age to put others' needs ahead of our own. For some, this is a religious principle (for example, it's what good Christians do). For others, it's simply part of being a good person; no church is involved. Let's take a closer look at this belief and the consequences of living it out.

Sometimes we need to put others first. Parents regularly put their children's well-being ahead of their own. And if one of your parents is dying, then both of their needs are probably more important than yours. But if the rest of the family is "too busy" to help, their needs are not necessarily more important. Chances are they're expecting you to pick up the slack. Of course, if you want to take leave from your job to be with your father during his final days, then do it. But do it because you want to be with him, or help your mother, or feel good about yourself after he's gone. Don't do it because your brothers and sisters expect you to.

When you're deciding what takes priority, it's important to be clear on something. Are you dealing with needs or desires? Your teenage daughter may "need" you to buy her an expensive dress, but you both know it's just a desire. Adults are equally capable of expressing wants as needs. They'll tell you they need to borrow money, they need your support or they need you to babysit. But usually if you don't give them what they "need", they'll survive. They'll find another way. Don't confuse desires, no matter how intense, with needs. They're not the same thing.

Even when you've made this distinction, it can still be hard to say *no*. Some people push our guilt buttons without even trying. Your neighbor's husband left her for another woman, and she's lost without him. How can you tell her you're too busy to help? Your brother makes less money than you do, and he supports three children on his salary. He borrows your lawn mower every weekend (and your snow blower whenever there's a storm). How can you ask him to pay for the gas?

There's a fine line between being kind and becoming a doormat. Maybe your brother helps you with other things, so there's a nice give and take. Or maybe he's in a tough spot right now, but he's working his way through it. On the other hand, maybe he takes your help for granted and never even considers contributing. One of the best indications is how you feel. If you're starting to resent your neighbor's demands on your time, then it's time to set some boundaries. If your brother is too busy to give you a hand now and then, perhaps he needs to be reminded of the importance of reciprocity. Think about the situation and notice how you feel. Most of the time, you'll know what you need to do.

Please don't misunderstand me. I'm not suggesting we shouldn't give more than we receive. People who are willing to help others, especially those who cannot give them anything in return, are some of the finest people in the world. I'm simply encouraging you to act according to your highest values. For me, helping someone to stand on his own is a great service; allowing someone to avoid responsibility is not. Making choices according to your highest values will give you the greatest sense of fulfillment.

Getting to Your Needs Later

Knowing what you need to do is the first step, but it's not the last. It can be tempting to keep putting others first; it keeps the flow of warm fuzzies coming in. People appreciate you. They don't know what they'd do without you.

Later never comes.

Not everyone gives up their personal time to feel needed or appreciated. Some of us do things for others because it feels like the right thing to do. We tell ourselves we'll get to our own needs later … but later never comes.

Valerie's mother taught her that there's always time to help someone in need. She has never asked whether there are limits to what she should do for others. Valerie is a wonderful daughter, sister, coworker and friend. She bakes all the cakes for family birthday parties. She's the one her siblings can count on to babysit. She'll look over a report or a proposal at work and offer detailed feedback, even for someone she hardly knows. And her friends know they can count on her for emotional support when things get tough.

Valerie is well-liked and respected. She's kind, generous and wise. And, at least on the surface, her boundaries seem healthy. She doesn't struggle with whether to lie for someone or take sides in a family dispute. No one would expect her to do something like that; they know she has strong values.

Valerie enjoys spending time with family and friends, but she can't remember the last time she could relax on her own. Whenever she sets aside some time for herself, something comes up. She tells herself that reading, listening to music or catching up on her favorite TV show will wait. And wait it does! Valerie feels vaguely unsatisfied, as if she's missing out on something.

Valerie's problem is a common one. She's turned her favorite role into an identity: the helpful, supportive woman. She thought she would find fulfilment through her relationships, but it isn't enough. Life is pushing Valerie to explore who she is beyond this role – and how to look after herself as well as others. She's being challenged to find that elusive balance.

How do we avoid falling into Valerie's trap? How do we respond when life offers us a similar challenge? There is no recipe for success, but I can suggest some guidelines.

First commit to some regular time for yourself (every week or on certain days of the week). Spend it doing something you enjoy, whether you're alone in your garden or spending time with a friend who doesn't need your support. If you've done that already, then move on to the next step: protect that time. If you're like Valerie, there's always something else to do. Learn to say that you're too busy or you'd love to do it another time. When there's a real need that can't be rescheduled, move something else so that you can still have your time to relax.

How much time you set aside is up to you. You can start with as little as half an hour a week if you need to. Whatever you start with, notice whether it's enough. If it isn't, keep increasing it until you get what you need.

In the beginning, you may want to spend that relaxation time with someone, so you'll have a commitment to keep. That way you'll be less likely to change your plans. Once you get used to protecting this time, you can start spending it alone, if that's what you want. You'll still have a commitment to keep – but this one will be to yourself.

If you can't find any time to relax, then you've taken on too much. Take a good look at your commitments. What is the purpose of each? Is that purpose being achieved? How valuable is it, and what are you giving up for it? Is it worth the cost? Some commitments cost money, while others seem free until you consider the time you're investing. Still others may carry a subtler cost, taking you out of integrity or leading you to feel used. Consider your options carefully, making sure your decisions are in alignment with your values.

Finally, let go of the idea that you can (or should) look after everyone all the time. Despite what you might think, this doesn't make you a good (or even happy) person – just a busy one. Besides … most people will manage without you. Anyone who "can't imagine getting through this without you" probably needs a better imagination. But I'm getting ahead of myself….

If You Don't Do It, No One Will

Susan checks her watch. No wonder the office is so quiet: it's almost 6:00. While she's packing up her laptop, her cellphone rings. It must be her husband, annoyed that she's not home making dinner. She answers absent-mindedly, preparing to apologize and offer to pick up some pizza on the way. She is surprised to hear a woman's voice on the other end of the phone.

"Susan, how are you? It's been a while."

It's her old customer Terri. Terri always said Susan was the only one in the company whom she could truly depend on. She had tried to get her assigned to her latest project, but Susan was already committed.

Yes, it has. What can I do for you, Terri?

"I'm sorry to bother you, Susan, but you're the only one I can count on."

Susan's first project deadline is a few short days away, and there's still no delivery date for a key piece of equipment.

"You know how important these deadlines are, Susan. I hate to ask, but I'm desperate. Would you please look into it for me in the morning?"

Susan sighs. She knows how difficult it is to pin down certain deliveries, and the company involved is notorious for bad paperwork. It will take hours to sort this out. But a customer needs her, and she wouldn't ask if it wasn't important.

Of course, Terri! Susan sounds happy to help. *Don't you worry about it another minute.*

"I knew I could count on you! Thanks a million! Enjoy your evening."

You too, Terri.

Susan calls for two pizza deliveries: one for home and one for the office.

In another part of town, Diane was talking to a nasty man. His son Jeremiah goes to school with her son, and she sees such potential in that little boy. He has this special quality, despite his background. (His mother died when he was born, and his father is an alcoholic.) Diane wants to see him succeed. With his father's permission, she enrolled him in an after-school program to help him with his studies.

His father had apparently decided his son shouldn't be the only one to benefit from Diane's generosity.

"I can't afford to keep sending Jeremiah to your after-school program. It's costing me too much in gas to pick him up; I have a very old car. If you want him to stay in the program, I need $500 a month."

She knew that the extra gas cost a fraction of that amount.

Give me the weekend to think about it. I'll get back to you on Monday.

Diane couldn't sleep. She loved that little boy. She so wanted to see him succeed!

32

By Monday morning, she had a plan.

Mr. Johnson, I'm calling about Jeremiah. I've spoken to several people at the after-school program, and it appears he's in danger of being dropped because you don't pick him up on time. I've also learned that there are several other students from your neighborhood enrolled in the program.

Diane made a simple proposal: The other parents had a car pool, which Jeremiah was welcome to join in exchange for one ride a week. Diane's nephew had his driver's license, and he would be happy to help.

Otherwise, Mr. Johnson, I'm afraid Jeremiah will be dropped from the program. And there's nothing I can do about it.

Diane had a choice: she could step up and help Jeremiah or, knowing she couldn't change his father, decide to let it go. Fortunately, she found a way to step up without being manipulated.

Susan also sees herself as stepping up – after all, a customer needs her. But is she really?

Let's listen in on the conversation between Susan and her boss, the very next day.

"Susan, I see you're having trouble keeping up with your deadlines. I know they're tight, but everyone is putting in extra time to make them, and I see from the log book that you are, too. What's the problem?"

Well, I've had some personal issues (referring to her friend who was calling every day with a crisis), *but I've taken care of that now. And then last night, I got a call from Terri ... you remember Terri?*

"Of course."

Well, she asked me to help with some equipment that's not being delivered on time. I couldn't say no to her. I thought it would take a few hours to track down, but my contact at the company is out sick, so it's taking much longer.

Her boss took a few moments to contemplate this.

"Susan, I took you off projects like Terri's because I thought you couldn't manage your time. The deadlines were met, but you were showing signs of stress. I thought you'd do better as a member of a team. Now I realize I didn't understand the problem.

"Taking on other people's responsibilities isn't the answer. Terri's project has a capable manager; Tom is one of the best. If you have a good contact at that supplier, or you understand their processes better than Tom, please share your information with him so that he can do his job more easily.

"But Susan, that's not even the real issue here. Based on your feedback, we strongly recommended avoiding that supplier. We found several workable alternatives, but Terri refused to budge. We accepted her choice with the understanding that we would not take on delivery problems. We have that in writing. We set a necessary boundary with specific consequences, and now you're allowing Terri to make her problems yours – and to some extent ours."

Susan is lucky; her boss is a good manager. Rather than getting angry, he's teaching her about communication and accountability. They call Terri together, and he tells her that Susan is not available to help her. He then instructs Susan, with Terri still on the line, to let him know if she receives any more such requests.

When they finish the call, Susan is looking down at her lap, fidgeting. She feels so foolish!

"Susan, I don't want you to feel badly about this. Just learn from it. Maybe some other time you'll get a call from a customer who really needs help. In that case, it's even more important to tell me about it. If someone is dropping the ball somewhere, I need to know. Otherwise it will keep happening, until we finally lose valuable business. Our customers shouldn't have to say, 'pretty please' to get good service from us."

Even when it's inconvenient,
doing the right thing doesn't bring you down.

Of course, there will be times when taking on someone else's responsibilities is the right thing to do. You just need to make your decision a conscious one. And if you're still not sure, try this simple test. Even when it's inconvenient, doing the right thing doesn't bring you down. If you feel angry or resentful about picking up the slack for someone, take some extra time to think. Maybe you're stressed or irritated, and it's really the right thing to do. Or maybe it's time to hold someone accountable.

They Can't Manage Without You

Some people surround themselves with friends and co-workers who seem to need constant support. These folks rely on them for all kinds of things: advice (about relationships, business decisions, what's best for their kids, even how to spend their money); emotional support; a loan until payday. The list never ends. Some find this exhausting; others admit they wouldn't know what to do without it.

Helplessness has a certain appeal, doesn't it? Women have been known to use it to manipulate men for as long as anyone can remember. It works best when the man wants to feel like a hero, the knight in shining armor who saves the damsel in distress. Of course, very few women (or men) are helpless; they simply find it easier to rely on others.

What gives, "I don't know what I'd do without you!" its power? Why do we keep doing things for others that they could learn to do for themselves?

Sometimes we allow people to depend on us because we think we must. Leaving them to fend for themselves would make us bad people. But encouraging unnecessary dependence is hardly noble. Sometimes the best way to help someone is to convince him to do something for himself. People often feel better about themselves when they succeed at something on their own.

Some of our reasons are less conscious. Doing things for others can make us feel special, particularly when the people we help feed our egos with lines like this:

"I really need your help. No one can run a fundraiser like you."

"Susie's party was so special. I don't know how you do it!"

"I can never thank you enough. I wouldn't have survived without you!"

"I knew I could count on you. You're a life saver!"

Even when these remarks are genuine, they may still serve to keep us hooked. It pays to notice how you feel at these times and ask yourself why you're doing something. If your principal reason is that the compliments feel good, you might want to reconsider.

Of course, we're often just helping a friend. In that case, go ahead and help. That's what friends are for. But if you're spending too much time that way, or if you're not feeling as warmly toward that friend as you once did, it may be time to do less.

Those of us who don't feel very good about ourselves often have another reason to help. When we don't expect to be loved, we often decide (consciously or not) to settle for being needed. That way we won't ever be alone. People who need to be needed encourage others to depend on them as much as possible. The more others rely on them, the more special and important they feel. But that insecurity never completely goes away.

If you suspect you're allowing others to depend on you too much, I encourage you to break the pattern. Get help if you need to. The truth is that they **can** manage without you. And you don't need their dependence, either. You've just gotten used to it.

You Can't Manage Without Them

Being depended upon is tricky because it can feel so good – and those good feelings, although short-lived, can be addictive. Being dependent on others is different. No one enjoys it, and the primary feeling associated with it is fear. That fear can be a powerful motivator.

The classic example of this is a woman who stays in a bad relationship because she believes she can't manage on her own. She thinks she needs her husband's money to survive. She wouldn't know what to do without him. But how often is that true?

Marie met Hal through her work; he was a manager and she was a secretary. He wasn't at all like the men she'd dated in the past. He wasn't in a hurry to move in with her. He impressed her with flowers, nice dinners and the occasional weekend away. Even after over six months (earlier relationships had ended in less than three), he didn't try to tell her how to dress or stop her from seeing her friends. When he proposed, Marie felt relieved. Already in her thirties, she thought she'd never find the right man.

On the day they announced their engagement, Hal told Marie she wouldn't work another day in her life. She missed her job at first, but when her son was born everything changed. She was a fantastic mother, and she was happy for a while.

Several years later, her marriage is empty. Marie's life is centered on her little boy. She adores him, and she loves looking after him. Getting a divorce would mean going back to work. She would have less time to devote to her son. And how would he cope with the change? No, no ... it's not possible.

But it **is** possible. It's just not very attractive. But neither is the current situation. Marie has a difficult choice to make. She can continue to see herself as a victim of circumstance, someone who's been dealt a bad hand. Or she can decide that she wants something better and figure out how to get it. Maybe there's hope for the relationship. She hasn't tried to change it, as she's been too fearful of the consequences. She and Hal have never even discussed what they want from their marriage. What if she tried? Maybe Hal would be willing to work with her to improve their relationship. He might surprise her.

If not, then Marie needs to understand her options. She knows the emotional cost of continuing in her current situation ... or does she? How often do we tell ourselves things aren't so bad because we're afraid to change? She must also know what life without her husband will cost – and where the money will come from. How much can she expect him to pay her each month? Will part-time work cover the difference? How much support can she realistically expect from family and friends? Some sacrifice will probably be necessary, but she won't know how much until she works out the numbers.

---

*You **can** manage without them.*

We seldom depend on others to survive. We may want what they have; we may even be miserable at the thought of living without it. But usually we can get what we want some other way – or live a good life regardless. We **can** "manage without them." It all comes down to whether we want it enough.

Good People Forgive and Forget

Saying "I'm sorry" doesn't make everything better. It's fine when you bump into someone, or when you're five minutes late for your lunch date. But sometimes "sorry" isn't enough.

At one of my talks, people were sharing their challenges with boundaries. It was a lively conversation with plenty of opinions being shared. Then a woman presented the following problem:

"My husband cheated on me. He's sorry and he swears he'll never do it again. I know I need to trust him again, but I don't know how."

Suddenly the room was still; this talkative bunch had nothing to say. I responded with some simple questions: *How do you know you need to trust him again? What has he done to earn that trust?*

This woman's husband was living a long distance away for his work. After the talk, she shared with me that when she suggested flying out to spend his birthday with him, he said *no*. I reminded her of what she already knew: that this was not a good sign. After the talk, she decided to surprise him and make the trip anyway. She discovered that he was living with another woman.

Trust must be earned.

It Won't Be Like This Forever

How often do we deal with something by telling ourselves it will be over soon? This may be a good approach to the flu, but it is not a healthy way to go through life.

Susan's husband comes home tired and cranky at the end of the day. Every day. The kids close their doors when he arrives – and have dinner at their friends' homes whenever they can. At first Susan tried to be light and cheerful, but that seemed to make things worse. So she gives him space to relax with a glass of wine and the newspaper. She tries not to make too much noise in the kitchen. But he never relaxes. She's walking on eggshells all night.

Why does Susan put up with this, night after night, month after month? And what about her husband? What keeps him at that job?

This scenario repeats itself five nights a week because neither Susan nor her husband is prepared to do what it takes to change things. Her husband has worked for the same company for over 20 years; he can't imagine going on interviews at his age. Every day, as he drives to the job he hates, he tells himself that things will change. "This used to be a great place," he thinks to himself. "Someday soon they'll fire that wretched management team and bring in someone who knows what he's doing. Then everything will go back to normal."

What her husband conveniently forgets each morning is that things have been this way for over two years, since the cutbacks began. This **is** normal.

Susan, on the other hand, has tried everything she can think of to make her husband happy. At first she made elaborate dinners, hoping good food would cheer him up. This meant doing most of the work the night before, as Susan also has a full-time job. Once it became clear that food wasn't the answer, she tried other approaches. Maybe if he had something to look forward to on the weekend … Maybe they could take a night off during the week to see a movie. Maybe he'd like to play poker with his friends. Or take up golf. Or something … anything …

But none of it worked. Her husband was in a negative environment all day long, and he didn't know how to shake it off long enough to enjoy himself. Until one of them faced the hard truth, the family would continue to live this way.

"When things get better" is a fairy tale. Things don't get better by themselves. They get better because someone's had enough and decides to do something about it.

There Must Be a Good Reason

We often put up with people's rudeness because we see them as good people having a bad day. We feel sorry for them. There must be some reason they're acting this way. We try to figure out what the problem is. (Maybe we can help.) In the meantime, the behavior only gets worse.

If your partner of five years suddenly becomes aggressive, trying to understand makes sense. You may be more concerned about his or her emotional state than the personal attack. You want to help. But if a colleague starts disrespecting you in front of others, the attacks are your main concern. You want to put a stop to them, the sooner the better.

Understanding can be useful –
but it isn't always necessary.

Understanding may be useful here, but mere contemplation is unlikely to provide it. You'll need to do something. You may decide to approach your colleague privately to find out what the problem is. Have you done something to offend him? What's the issue? If you can clear it up, then your immediate problem is solved. You may, however, want to set a boundary for the future.

You may also decide that understanding isn't necessary. You may let your colleague know that he's completely out of line, and you won't tolerate it. You may do this publicly, when it happens, or privately, after you've had some time to cool off. It all depends on you. My own approach would be to set the boundary right away (politely but firmly) Then I'd follow up in private to find out if there's a misunderstanding or other problem to deal with. But if you don't know what to say in the moment, or if you believe a confrontation wouldn't be in your best interest, you may prefer to handle it afterwards, when you've had some time to think.

More often than not, trying to understand someone you're not close to is a useless mental exercise. It keeps your mind spinning around, wondering, without the information it needs to draw a conclusion. And it keeps your focus away from yourself and your response. You end up feeling helpless and confused. It may be easier to break this habit once you understand a few things:

1. It isn't possible to understand everyone.
2. It isn't possible to understand anyone all the time. Human beings are complex, and there will always be things we don't know about them.
3. The need to understand is a trick of the mind. Understanding may help – or it may not – but it isn't necessary.

Everyone has reasons for the things they do. And the reasons are always good ones, according to them. Otherwise they would have made different choices. But they may not be good enough for you. Greed is a common reason for lying, cheating or stealing. If someone cheated you, would the fact that she was driven by greed make it OK?

Put your focus where it belongs. If the problem is that someone you care about is in pain, then focus there. If the problem is that someone isn't respecting you or your boundaries, then focus on how to respond. Make your boundary clear, and be prepared to make it stick. Do it with respect, and you'll have nothing to regret.

It Will Be Worth the Sacrifice Later

Society teaches us to sacrifice for the future. We have savings accounts and retirement plans for exactly that reason. A little bit of sacrifice, repeated often enough, can pay for our children's education or fund that dream trip to Hawaii. And that's a good thing.

But not all sacrifices are equal. There are three important questions to ask yourself when considering any significant sacrifice:

1. What is the payoff?
2. How certain is the outcome?
3. Is it worth the price?

The answer to the first question seems a bit obvious, doesn't it? Of course you know what you're sacrificing for! But do you really?

Now that Steve has started his first job, he's found an apartment near the office. He shares it with two loud, messy roommates, so he doesn't spend much time there. He chose this apartment because the rent was low and he could save even more money by walking to work in good weather. Steve wants a place of his own, and keeping his expenses down will make that possible sooner. He calculated that he'd save $300 a month on rent, utilities and transportation, so he decided to go for it.

So what's the catch? The payoff seems clear, and Steve decided it was worth the price. But it's not so simple.

Since he hardly spends any time at home, Steve could save some money by choosing a much smaller place than he originally imagined. The rent and utilities would still be higher, and it would cost him more to get to work. The added cost would be only $200 a month, $100 less than he originally calculated.

But that's not all. Let's see how Steve is spending all that time away from home. He's hanging out in sports bars, eating out and going out with friends – all things he would do anyway, but not nearly so often. When Steve compares the social life he wants with the one he's using to avoid his roommates, he finds out that he's spending most of that $200 savings on things he doesn't value much.

He's lucky if he's saving $50 a month. That doesn't bring him much closer to a place of his own.

Steve didn't understand the payoff; an extra $50 a month is not what he bargained for. And it's not worth the price. Steve resents his roommates, and he has nowhere to relax at the end of the day. He's also gaining weight from all those nights out. He decides to rent a small apartment in a complex with an onsite gym. That extra $50 is money well spent.

Sometimes we understand the payoff perfectly, but we misunderstand the price. Karen just got divorced, and her parents encouraged her to move in with them for a while. They're happy to let her stay with them for a few years while she saves her money for a down payment on a house. Karen wants to live in one of the most expensive parts of town, so she quickly agrees. The payoff is clear, and it's reasonably certain. All that's left to consider is the price.

Karen has always done her best to look after her parents, even when she was married and living more than two hours away. Now that she's in their home, her mother expects a lot more of her. Doing most of the housework isn't an issue for Karen; she's grateful for the opportunity to keep her expenses down. She's even offered to pay the utility bills or buy the groceries for the three of them, but her mother will have nothing of that. "My darling, you need to save everything you can for that beautiful home of yours. We're only too happy to help!"

Unfortunately, her mother's financial generosity comes at an emotional price. Every evening over dinner, she grills Karen on the details of her day. During the week, she wants to know everything that's happening at the office. On the weekend, she wants to know all about Karen's friends – especially the men. Karen values her privacy, while her mother sees no need for it. She also finds subtle ways to remind Karen of the debt she's accumulating.

Sharing every detail of her life is only the beginning. Karen's mother looks forward to spending weekends with her daughter in that beautiful home. And she speaks as though she'll be playing an active role in the decision-making process: "You probably don't remember this, but I've always been very interested in real estate trends. I'll make sure you invest in the right area."

After a few weeks, Karen realizes that the favor she has accepted has some serious strings attached. She'll need to decide how much she's willing to give in exchange for that "free" rent.

It's Just One Little Thing

"Why won't you do this one little thing for me? What's the big deal?"

"Why won't you help me? You know I'd do it for you."

"It's just this once...."

Guilt is a powerful motivator.

It's easy to feel bad when someone wants a "small favor" and you don't want to do it. You can feel selfish, ungrateful, or just plain mean. (And if you don't feel that way on your own, someone may be more than happy to give you a little push.) Before you know it, you're overwhelmed with guilt.

Because guilt is such a powerful motivator, it's important to understand this "one little thing." Is it as small as you think? Is there only one thing involved?

Sometimes the favor seems small, but it's part of a larger pattern. If someone expects you to drop what you're doing whenever he needs something, then his expectations – and his disrespect for you and your time – are anything but small. Once you see that, "What's the big deal?" is no longer such a difficult question.

Often people use ugly tactics to get what they want. Guilt trips, the threat of rejection, intimidation – these methods are offensive. You would be wise to say *no* to these tactics, regardless of the demands attached to them. Saying *yes* is the fastest way to ensure more of the same. As a client of mine once pointed out, we teach people how to treat us. She was so right.

Sometimes what's being presented as a little thing is simply unreasonable. Taking someone shopping for an entire day is a lot to ask. You may have other plans for your weekend, and all that shopping may be too much for you. "You know I'd do it for you," doesn't mean much coming from your friend the shopaholic. If you asked her to do something she finds unpleasant, and stick it out for the entire day, "I'd do it for you," would vanish into thin air.

Finally, no request is small if it involves sacrificing your integrity. Even a little bit. When your values are at stake, "just this once" is once too many.

It's Worth It to Keep the Peace

How often do you put up with something (rude remarks, unreasonable expectations, etc.) just to keep the peace? We tell ourselves that there's no harm in this one favor, or that she didn't mean to be so rude, or that it's not worth fighting over. And sometimes it isn't. So how do you know when to stand up for yourself and when to go with the flow?

Let your feelings and common sense be your guide. If a remark doesn't affect you much, then there's probably no need to respond. And if it's the first time this person has said something like this, you may decide to wait and see whether it happens again. But if it's becoming a pattern and you keep thinking about it, or if you're expected to do something you don't want to, then it may be time to respond. Say *no* to the favor, or let the person know that you don't like what he's saying. Say it out loud and see what happens. As long as you don't engage in personal attacks, things should improve.

If the problem continues, then decide what you want to do about it. (And, no, hoping it will go away is not an option.) Do you need to be around this person? If not, then your problem is easily solved. Otherwise, consider ending the conversation at the first sign of trouble. "You know how I feel about this topic," or "I'm not going to discuss it again," should do the trick.

"Keeping the peace" is a funny thing. Often the peace you're referring to is merely the appearance of peace, a lack of overt conflict. The tension may be so thick you can cut it with a knife. There's nothing peaceful about that.

And what price are you paying for this so-called peace? There's a conflict within you: part of you wants to stand up for yourself, and part of you wants to avoid confrontation. This inner conflict is usually more painful than the outer one could ever be.

If something's not OK with you, it's important to respect yourself enough to deal with it, even if you feel uncomfortable speaking up. After all, if you don't show yourself some respect, who will?

There's Nothing You Can Do About It

"She'll never change, so why bother?"

Diane has had enough … again. She asked her mother to look after the children while she and her husband attended a friend's wedding. She made it clear that they were to play outside, even though they would rather watch TV or play video games. She and her husband returned from the wedding about half an hour early – to find her mother baking her second batch of cookies and the children in the living room, watching people running from an explosion.

Her mother had the usual excuses. Diane felt the usual anger, resentment and helplessness.

Diane wants her children to spend quality time with their grandmother, like she did when she was growing up. If her mother would respect her rules – actually, if she would just respect her position as their mother – then everything would be fine. But her mother sees no problem with TV or video games, and she feels completely justified in ignoring such "silly" rules.

If Diane had come home a few minutes later, the children would have been happily munching their cookies in front of the TV. Instead, Diane threw them in the trash, calling her mother a few choice names in the process. She finished by shouting, "You never change, do you?!!"

Nothing will change until you do.

Diane has a point. Her mother hasn't changed a bit – nor will she. But her mother's stubbornness is not the reason she feels angry and helpless. She created those feelings herself, through her own form of stubbornness.

Diane keeps asking her mother to babysit, telling herself that this time will be different. This time her mother will take the children outside and play with them. It's a beautiful day, and she won't want to lose them to the TV set.

She refuses to face reality. Her mother bonds with the children by baking them cookies; she isn't going to give that up in favor of taking them outside to play. She's not that kind of grandmother.

Diane doesn't want to give up her fantasy of the children playing games with their grandmother in the backyard, like she did with her grandparents when she was their age. But like most fantasies, it doesn't match reality. She has two choices: accept Grandma's cookies and TV or find someone else to watch them. Her mother won't change, and neither will the situation – until Diane changes. She's the one who wants a different outcome, and it's up to her to make it happen.

What about that dream of playing in the backyard? There's nothing to stop her from playing catch with the kids – and inviting Grandma to join them. If she doesn't want to play, maybe she'd enjoy watching. You never know until you try.

You Just Can't Say No to Someone

Many of us are pretty good at setting boundaries ... except with that one person. Often it's a parent or employer. Sometimes it's a friend or acquaintance with an air of authority. Or perhaps you know someone who "just won't take *no* for an answer." These people seem stronger than we are. They consistently get what they want, regardless of our otherwise firm boundaries. They know how to get to us.

Linda stands to greet her mother, who is fashionably late for their lunch date. She forces a smile, wondering what she'll talk her into this time. Investing in her uncle's latest business venture? Chairing another fundraising committee? Spending a weekend afternoon giving business advice to someone who will never use it? She's done all of this and more at her mother's insistence. What does she have in store for her today?

Ten minutes later, after catching up on all the family gossip, Linda takes a deep breath. "So ... what did you want to talk about? You said it was important."

"Yes, I did...." She pauses.

"You know your brother's struggling to find work...." She pauses again.

Linda can't remember the last time her mother looked uncomfortable about anything. Her heart races. What could she want from her?

"He's tried everything, you know."

Linda doubts that. Her mother could never face the truth about her only son. She nods and mumbles, "It's tough in this economy."

"Exactly. That's why he needs your help...."

There's that pause again. And that uncomfortable look. Linda grips the table to steady herself.

"Just say it, Mom. What does he want from me? You know I can't get him a job."

"I know. We've all tried.... Linda, he's running out of money. He needs a place to stay – just until he gets back on his feet."

Linda looks at her mother in stunned silence.

"He just needs a place to eat and sleep. He won't be in your way. He'll be out looking for a job most of the time."

"Mom ..."

"He needs his family now. You're his sister. You can't let him down."

"I ... I can't ..."

"Of course you can. You must. He's your family. There's nothing more important than family. I'll let your brother know that you'll be ready for him at the end of the month."

Linda doesn't know what to say. Her mother is right; he is family. She can never argue with her mother's logic.

How do you deal with someone like this? What do you do when you can't come up with an argument, but you can't afford to give in?

Your first step is to take your time. Don't make any decisions while you're feeling emotional. You will only think clearly when you've had some time away. When others insist on a decision, put it off. Make, "I need to think about this," your mantra.

When your head clears and you're deciding how to respond, keep this in mind:

> **You have the right to make your own decisions, based on your own values and beliefs. Other people's logic is based on their values and beliefs. It's important to know the difference.**

For example, here's what Linda's mother had to say:

You must do this because he's your family – and there's nothing more important than family.

This may be compelling to anyone who believes that family is important. But its real power lies not in the speaker's statements, but in the listener's failure to question them, to consider them from her own point of view. Let's look at Linda's perspective:

My brother is unemployed because he's lazy.

I don't want to support that laziness by giving him a free place to stay.

And I certainly don't want him in my space.

Instead of fighting her mother's perspective, Linda needs to look at the problem from many perspectives. She can consider everything from her mother's desires to her own her feelings and beliefs to the practical reality of the situation. What will happen if she says *yes*? What will happen if she says *no*? What other options are there? Is there a way that she can support him while still encouraging him to be responsible for himself?

No Is a Bad Word

Every time you say *yes* to one thing, you say *no* to another. You just haven't said it out loud. Some of us feel like failures unless we're saying *yes*. But is it possible to say *yes* to everyone – and everything? Saying *yes* to a lie can mean saying *no* to your integrity. Saying *yes* to spending Saturday night with your sister means saying *no* to spending it with your friends. Life is full of these conflicts; for every spoken *yes*, there's at least one implied *no* – often more.

I once had a client for whom *no* was truly a bad word. Based on childhood experiences, she associated it with judgment and rejection. She found rejection painful, and she didn't want to hurt anyone she cared for that way. Because she equated *no* with intense emotional pain, she was unwilling to say it.

If you struggle with this simple little word, you're not alone. Here are a few things to keep in mind when your fears surface:

- Your fear is a learned response. There's nothing inherently wrong with the word *no*, or with setting healthy boundaries.
- Those who find any kind of refusal hurtful need to heal their wounds. Protecting them from pain is not your responsibility – nor is it best for them in the long run.
- Boundaries protect what's important to you: your privacy, your integrity, your family time. Without boundaries, you won't be able to enjoy the things you value the most.

Before saying *yes*, be clear about what matters to you. Would you be saying *no* to something important? If so, how might you meet your own needs as well as those of your friends or family? If you're not willing to look after your brother's kids for the weekend, could you still help? Maybe a few family members can pitch in. Could you look after them Saturday morning and take them to their grandparents after lunch? There may be many things you can say *yes* to and still protect the time you need for other priorities. Pairing your *no* with a meaningful *yes* lets your brother know that he's still important to you. You're not saying *no* to him (or what matters to him); you're just limiting your commitment. That way you can say *yes* to him without having to say *no* to yourself.

Sometimes you need to say *no* in order to say *yes*. And often that's what's best for everyone.

Don't Believe Everything You Think!

Although our beliefs and expectations are formed over a lifetime, most of them came into being when we were young. The process was primarily an unconscious one. Some beliefs came straight from our parents and other authority figures, while others resulted from our own experiences. Pain and pleasure are powerful teachers. Some of our beliefs are nothing more than the conclusions we came to before we were old enough to read and write! Others are embedded in the very fabric of our culture. But that doesn't mean that they're true.

Question your beliefs. Question what others tell you, and question what you tell yourself. *Is that true? Does it really mean what I think it means?* It is only by asking the right questions that we find meaningful answers.

Once you understand yourself and deal with the half-truths that have kept you stuck, it's time to look at what you're really saying when you set that boundary. In the next chapter, you'll learn the eight communication mistakes that can destroy your boundaries. Which ones are you making?

3RD CHAPTER

WHAT ARE YOU REALLY SAYING?

For many, communication is the hardest part of boundary-setting. We know where to draw the line; we're clearly within our rights and comfortable with the decision. But we struggle with putting it into words, or we don't know how to respond when someone challenges us.

The second book in this series, *7 Easy Ways to Say NO to Almost Anyone*, addresses these conversations in detail, offering many ways to express yourself. Here we're going to look at the most common communication problems, those that prevent us from gracefully setting and maintaining our boundaries.

Not Making Sure Your Boundary Is Understood

Steve is starting to wonder whether he'll ever have a life of his own. His parents have been showing up at his apartment unannounced. No matter how much he hints that he needs to get some things done, they insist on taking him to lunch and stay for hours afterwards. Now his aunts and uncles are doing the same. He's missing his time with his friends, who get together every Saturday for lunch at their favorite sports bar. He won't talk to his parents directly, as he's afraid of his mother's reaction. So instead, he brings up the issue at a family picnic, when his parents, aunts and uncles are all together. Everyone is very supportive of his need for notice, and Steve heaves a sigh of relief. He wishes he had done this sooner.

Imagine Steve's shock when his parents arrive at 11:00 on Saturday morning, just as he's getting ready to leave for the sports bar.

"What are they doing here?" he wonders. "Don't they remember what I said?"

When he delicately questions them, he learns that they remember quite well. His mother assures him that his aunts and uncles completely understand, and they'll call ahead in the future. "I'm so glad you got that straightened out!"

Steve didn't even consider the possibility that his parents would exclude themselves from his request. When he hinted about his needs at the picnic, one of his aunts caught on and suggested that they all needed to call ahead. He assumed that his parents got the message, too. Clearly they did not.

Sometimes we assume that others understand the unspoken details of our requests. "Please don't call me late in the evening," may mean after 11:00 to some and after 8:00 to others. If you don't want to start a conversation after 8:00, then say so. They may also misunderstand the reasons – and therefore the context. "I'm too busy to join the Women's League," may be interpreted as, "Ask me again once this deadline is over." The real meaning is lost: "My job and my family take up all of my time. I'm not joining any social organizations." If that's what you mean, then say so. Chances are the requests will stop.

If you're dealing with something more difficult to explain, such as what you consider private or how much help you're willing to give, then be specific. For example:

Please don't share what I tell you about my love life with the rest of the family. It's OK if you tell them how well I'm doing financially, but I don't want them hearing about my relationships.

I'd be happy to help you if you tell me a few days ahead of time, but I can't do anything for you on such short notice.

I won't do it for you, but I'd be happy to tell you how it's done. If you get stuck, you can call me in the evening and I'll help you sort out any problems.

Finally, check for signals. If someone is nodding too quickly or seems distracted, your message may not stick. You could ask a friend to restate your boundary in his own words. "I want to be sure I've made myself clear; what will you do next time?" Or you could refocus his attention (or pause until the distraction passes), then repeat your boundary.

Sending the Wrong Message

When you set a boundary, you're telling someone what's OK and what isn't. If you want to convey that you really mean it, look the person straight in the eye while you're talking. Speak in an even, firm tone of voice. Don't hesitate. Don't smile or laugh. And don't look down or away. These actions send the message that you're not comfortable with your boundary. You might want it, but you don't think you're entitled to it – so you're not likely to defend it. When you appear insecure, people don't take your boundary seriously.

What if you don't want to seem too serious? Maybe you're talking to someone who respects you and your boundaries; you simply need to make this one clear. Then you can use your usual friendly tone, and you don't need to look the person straight in the eye. Just don't look down or away – unless that's what's expected in your culture.

If your boundary isn't negotiable, you may not want to ask whether the other person agrees with you. ("That's only fair, right?") Some people will be happy to disagree. The same goes for asking permission. Approaching a difficult colleague with, "Is it OK if we move our meeting to next week?" suggests that moving the meeting is a preference. You're flexible. If that's true, then go ahead and ask. Just be prepared for the possibility of attending the meeting as scheduled.

If your decision is made, why not consider a different approach? State it in a matter-of-fact tone, as if it's the most natural thing in the world: "One of my clients needs me to handle a crisis, so I can't make our meeting tomorrow. Can we reschedule for next week?" Then discuss alternatives: "My first available time is 3:00 on Wednesday. If we need to meet sooner, I'll see what I can do to change my schedule." This lets your colleague know that you won't be there at the scheduled time – and that her needs are also important to you.

Sending the message that you're comfortable with your decision (and expecting others to be as well) gives your boundary a solid foundation. Others are far less likely to challenge you when they see that you're serious.

Making Excuses

Sometimes we weaken our boundaries by saying too much. We want to be liked; we want to feel understood. We're looking for approval. So we explain our choices, hoping others will give us what we want:

"Of course I understand! Don't give it another thought!"

"I had no idea you were so busy! I'm sure I can find someone else to help."

"Naturally your family comes first. Another time, then."

Not everyone wants what's best for you.

When you're dealing with people who genuinely care about you, this approach usually works. The person who wanted something from you understands that something else is more important right now. You've set your boundary in a way that respects your relationship; there are no hard feelings.

So why not do this all the time? Because not everyone wants what's best for you. You know who these people are. When dealing with them, excuses and justifications aren't just unnecessary – they're counterproductive. They open the door to endless debate. These people will do their utmost to convince you that you can do everything they've asked of you. By the end of it all, you'll probably feel both exhausted and resentful. But that won't stop them – this time or the next.

Another popular time for excuses is when we don't want to tell the truth. Lisa's old friend from college wants to see her favorite band. They're playing at a bar in town. Lisa no longer goes to bars; she doesn't like the drinking or the smoke. She's afraid to say that to her friend, who still goes bar-hopping on weekends. Instead she makes excuses:

> *It's been a long week. I'm too tired to go out on Friday night.*
> "No problem. We can go on Saturday."
> *I have plans on Saturday.*
> "You can change your plans. They're only here for one weekend!"
> *I don't know ...* (already running out of excuses)
> "We'll go on Friday, then! You'll be home by 10:30 – plenty of time to rest!"

Lisa ends up going to hear the band with her friend. And although the music was nice, she wished she was home watching TV. And no matter how long she stayed in the shower, it seemed she could still smell the smoke in her hair.

It's important to remember that approval has its price. Don't let yourself be talked into things that don't work for you. Your best approach is to be honest with those you care about and consider a simple "No, thank you," for everyone else. You don't need a "good excuse" to do what's right for you.

Not Explaining Your Reasons

As mentioned earlier, saying too much can backfire. Explanations give manipulative people points to argue, and their persistence is often stronger than your resolve. But when you're dealing with people who care about you, whom you trust to take your needs into account, then explanations can support your cause.

The obvious benefit of explanations is that they help you to get things done. If it's your turn to take the kids home from soccer practice, then a friend who needs your advice can meet you for coffee beforehand – preferably near the soccer field.

But explanations are good for relationships in other ways. Your explanation (or lack of one) influences the stories in people's heads. Consider Valerie, who recently realized that she needs to look after herself more. She decided to turn off her phone on Friday nights, as she was tired by the end of the week. When she told her friends, most of them were supportive. But her closest friend was hurt. Ellen was between boyfriends, and she missed being taken to dinner or a movie at the end of the week. That Friday night phone call took away the loneliness. She thought Valerie was being selfish; obviously she didn't care about her as much as she thought.

Soon Valerie sensed a problem. When she sat with Ellen and told her how exhausted she felt by Friday afternoon, her friend's attitude changed. She saw Valerie as worn out rather than uncaring. She asked if she could call her later in the evening if she was **really** lonely, and Valerie agreed that she could call after 8:30. The phone rang at precisely 8:30 for the first two weeks, and then it stopped. Ellen wanted Valerie to have her quiet time, and she realized that she needed to get out and do something on Fridays. She found other friends to socialize with, and Valerie had her quiet time.

Explanations also serve another practical purpose. People who care about you are more likely to remember – and therefore respect – your boundary when they understand its intention. Tell them what you're protecting, and they'll be happy to help.

For example, asking your friends not to call before noon should lead to fewer morning phone calls, especially in the beginning. But after a while, well-meaning people may forget. If you explain that this is your creative time, and that you can't meet your deadlines without it, they're more likely to remember. They'll imagine you making sketches or composing music – or whatever it is that you do – and won't want to disturb you. They won't want anyone else to disturb you, either. Now that they understand, they may even help you to protect what matters to you.

Not Wanting to Repeat Yourself

"If I've told you once, I've told you a thousand times …"

How many parents have said this to their children? And how often? We repeat things to children because they're important. The fact that they didn't listen the first time (or at least didn't remember) doesn't make the information matter less. We don't give up after a few tries and decide that our kids are going to play with matches whether we like it or not.

And yet, many of us do this all the time with adults. We resent people for ignoring our boundaries, but we don't want to repeat them. We're afraid to be rude. But if your boundary is reasonable, then who's the rude one?

Sometimes we just need to get over our fear and repeat ourselves – as often as needed. Of course, you **can** find another way to express your boundary. That way you won't feel like a broken record. But I recommend using the exact same words - every time. Because that tells them you mean it.

Try it for yourself. Imagine someone wants to borrow money from you, and you've already refused. Compare these two conversations; feel free to read them out loud if it helps:

"Won't you lend me $20? I'm broke."

I'm sorry, but I'm not lending you any more money.

"Please … I really need it."

I don't have any more money to lend.

"But I'm desperate. I'll pay you back as soon as I get my check."

I can't afford it.

"It's only $20. And I really, really need it. You'll have it back next Friday."

I just can't do it.

"Sure you can. Come on, be a pal ... you always have some spare cash."

Please stop pushing me.

"I wouldn't push if I didn't really need it. And you know you can afford it. Please? I really need your help ..."

That conversation was without repetition. Here's the same one with it:

"Won't you lend me $20? I'm broke."

I'm sorry, but I'm not lending you any more money.

"Please ... I really need it."

I said I'm not lending you any more money.

"But I'm desperate. I'll pay you back as soon as I get my check."

I said I'm not lending you any more money.

"It's only $20. I really, really need it. And you'll have it back next Friday."

How many times must I tell you that I'm not lending you any more money?

What did you notice about the first conversation? When we try to avoid repetition, we often end up making excuses ("no more money to lend" or "I can't afford it"), which leads to pointless debate. When you're not afraid to repeat yourself, it's easier to stick with your *no*. You don't need to come up with new ways of saying the same thing, and no excuses means there's less room for argument. It also means that you don't need to bend the truth to suit your needs. And repetition makes your boundary stronger. The second set of responses has more impact than the first.

Of course, you don't need to continue either conversation as long as I did in these examples. Once your boundary is ignored, feel free to walk away:

"Won't you lend me $20? I'm broke."

I'm sorry, but I'm not lending you any more money.

"Please ... I really need it."

I said I'm not lending you any more money. See you tomorrow [walking away or hanging up the phone].

If the topic comes up again, you can take it one step further: *I told you I'm not lending you any more money. Please don't ask me again.*

Following Someone Else's Lead

"Lisa, don't forget your sister's birthday. We're going to that fancy restaurant – you know, her favorite. Be there by seven."

Dad, you know how I feel about that restaurant. I told you I wouldn't go back there.

"Don't worry, I'll get them to make something special for you."

You tried that last time, Dad. It was a disaster. Sarah knows I won't go back.

"Do you always have to be so selfish? Why can't you put your family first for a change?"

How can you call me selfish? I practically raised my sister, and she can't even take my needs into account when she chooses a restaurant!

"So you did your duty when your mother was sick. Must everything you do come with a price tag?"

A price tag?! How can you say that? I've never asked for anything in return – except maybe a little respect!

"Respect??? Look who's talking about respect! You don't know the meaning of the word! If you want to stay a member of this family, you will go to your sister's dinner!"

I'm not a child. Don't you dare order me around!

What's gone wrong here? How did things get so ugly?

Don't lose control of the conversation.

61

Lisa tried to set a boundary, which her family ignored. When she maintained it, her father attacked. And that's where Lisa lost control of the conversation. She spent the rest of it reacting to whatever her father said with angry, hurtful remarks.

If you're struggling to make your boundary stick, this is not the time to let someone else control the interaction. Before you know it, that person will be controlling you. (Who was in control of Lisa's emotions: Lisa or her father?) Here are a few of the ways people might try to control you:

Personal attacks. This tactic is popular when you've just caught someone crossing your clearly stated boundary. Personal attacks trigger anger and indignation. This shifts the conversation from the other to you. If you defend yourself long enough, or hard enough, you may never get around to taking whatever action is necessary.

Guilt. People who use guilt regularly soon become masters of the judgmental look and the carefully chosen phrase. ("Must everything you do come with a price tag?") Once you're hooked, it's all downhill. If this happens to you while trying to set or maintain a perfectly reasonable boundary, then it's time to take control. Stop paying attention to the guilt trip and ask yourself, "What do I need to do right now? How do I make this boundary stick?" Maybe you need to create consequences for a boundary crossed. Maybe you need to walk away from someone who's trying to take advantage of you. Or maybe you need to think about your options before you act. Don't let guilt distract you from doing what's best for you.

Demands. Another common tactic is to make demands. For example, I could demand justification for your position: "What gives you the right …?" Before responding, ask yourself one important question: Whose decision is this? Does this person have authority over you? Is he or she entitled to a say in the matter? If not, then ignore this distraction. Set or maintain your boundary and move on.

When it comes to family, staying calm can be a real challenge. They know exactly how to push your buttons. If your emotions are too intense to control, consider walking away. You can continue the conversation another time – or choose not to discuss it again. Walking away can also give you time to reconsider your boundary. Maybe there's something you can find to eat at that restaurant after all. Or maybe it's time to have a chat with your sister. If there's a problem in an important relationship, see if you can deal with it. Then you won't have so many boundaries to argue about.

Don't let someone lead you into the kind of argument that no one wins. Take control of the situation and do what's best for you.

Being Afraid of Silence

How often have you given in to someone even though the other person didn't say a word? Silence is a powerful weapon.

What makes it so powerful? Nothing more than our imaginations. Do you think others are quiet because they're busy agreeing with you? Of course not. You imagine the worst: He's too angry to speak. She thinks I'm stupid – it's written all over her face.

The power of silence as a weapon comes directly from its victim. When we interpret silence as judgment and react by judging ourselves, we give the silent one power over us. We want to avoid feeling guilty, or undeserving, so we speak. We defend ourselves so that the silence – and the awful feelings that come with it – will end. Any sign of approval or agreement, no matter how small, will relieve the tension.

As long as you suffer with the notion that you're not good enough, others can use that against you without saying a word. A look, a grunt, even a total lack of response can trigger those painful feelings. It is not the silence that controls you. It isn't even the feelings triggered by the silence. It is your fear of those feelings that keeps you trapped. It drives you to make others happy so that you can feel better for a moment. If it weren't for the fear, you'd be free.

If you don't know how to calm that fear, maybe you can learn to reinterpret silence. Silence can mean many things; the most common reason for it is contemplation. Sometimes we just need to think. So take a deep breath. Nothing terrible will happen while you wait. I promise.

Being Too Polite

Many of us were brought up to believe that you can never be too polite. That may be true when you're asking for a favor. But at other times, being polite can be limiting – especially if you have a narrow definition of the term.

To many people, being polite means not saying or doing anything that those around them might find unpleasant. It means nodding their heads even though they disagree, or going along with things that feel uncomfortable. It means not speaking their truth.

People who live this way usually feel empty inside. They're also targets for manipulators, as they seldom stand up for themselves. So what do you do? If being polite is important to you, how do you avoid losing yourself in the process?

Don't be polite. Be respectful.

It's simple, really. Instead of being polite, be respectful. In all your interactions, insist on respecting both yourself and others. Expect to be treated with respect as well.

Let's see how we might apply this principle to some difficult situations. Your mother wants you to host another family get-together. Rather than telling her you'd like someone else to do it, you make excuses about being too busy. She keeps asking, and the tension is building. Eventually you feel as though you have no choice and set a date. This pattern will continue, every few months, until you speak your truth: "Mom, it's time someone else did the hosting. It takes my whole day, and I feel exhausted afterwards. This time I just want to show up with my pot luck dish and enjoy myself." When others ask too much of you, it's important to let them know. Don't expect them to figure it out for themselves.

Maureen has looked after her younger brother all her life. He's a master of the guilt trip. Today he wants his big sister to loan him money for concert tickets. They'll be sold out by the end of the day, and his credit card is maxed out. She's tired of being his personal banker, and he often takes two or three months to pay her back. When he wants to borrow money, she refuses … at first. After a few minutes of guilt, she gives in. Maureen was brought up to be polite no matter what; she's never called him on his use of guilt because it would be rude. If she were to use respect as her guide, her decision would be clear. She could say any one of a number of things:

I'm not comfortable lending you any more money.

I'm not lending you any more money. You'll need to manage your finances without my help.

I'm not going to feel guilty because you haven't saved enough money to pay for a concert. The answer is still no.

In the past, I've lent you money because I've felt guilty. I'm not doing that again. I want that money for other things … and I'm not discussing it any further.

In a different situation, you might want time to think. If you're conflicted, you may want to make sure that you aren't making a bad decision just to avoid feeling guilty. Something like this might work:

I need time to think about this. I'll let you know tomorrow.

All of these responses are respectful. Notice that, even when guilt is mentioned, there are no accusations. Accusations give others points to argue and reasons to get defensive. This is a recipe for conflict, something polite people usually want to avoid. But if you're willing to risk the conflict, you may want to be more direct about the tactics being used:

Please stop trying to make me feel guilty. This isn't my responsibility.

If you want my help, you'll need to show me why this is the best solution – not what will happen if I don't come to the rescue.

The choice is yours. Having good manners doesn't mean putting up with someone else's bad ones. Being polite is about the way you convey your message: your tone of voice, avoiding blame and labeling, etc. If something needs to be said, you can still say it. Don't let anyone tell you that it's impolite to mention the elephant in the room!

Accept the Challenge

Communicating our boundaries can be a real challenge. So many emotions come into play that it's hard to think straight. Get to know yourself; understand the traps that you fall into most easily. Learn to recognize the triggers. Take a deep breath – or two or three – and decide what to do next.

If you're too emotional, then take a break. Give yourself the time you need to think clearly. Don't let others rush you into a decision or make it for you.

If you think your emotions are making it difficult to set good boundaries, then the next chapter is for you. Read it and learn the eight ways your emotions can hijack your decisions – sometimes without you even knowing it.

4ᵀᴴ CHAPTER

ARE YOUR EMOTIONS RUNNING THE SHOW?

I magine Monday morning starting like this:
"I can't go to work this morning; I can't let people see me like this. I need you to call my boss."
And say what? That you can't work today because you're hung over?
"Make up something. I can't go in like this; I'll lose my job. Then what'll we do?"
How can you do this to me? You know how much I hate to lie!
What are you willing to do for fear? Which values are more important, and which ones vanish when you're faced with such a painful emotion?

Some people are afraid of confrontation; the fear it evokes is overwhelming. Some can't handle embarrassment, as it quickly turns to humiliation. And others succumb at the first sign of guilt. This short-term focus creates long-term problems. The price we pay for avoiding that pain in the moment is more moments just like it. By trying to avoid the problem, we perpetuate it. We teach people that they can use our fear to control us.

Start by taking small risks and learning that these emotions won't kill you. Standing up for yourself has another benefit, one that's especially relevant here: it feels much better than being a doormat. There's one unpleasant feeling that you won't need to experience again!

Fear of Confrontation

I doubt that anyone enjoys confrontation. Arguments are unpleasant, and some people are harder to disagree with than others. That's because they make things personal. They take any complaint or criticism as a personal attack and retaliate. They raise their voices; they threaten; they blame everyone except themselves. For everything. I call these people *intimidators*.

People who lack confidence in themselves tend to be afraid of intimidators, as their tirades trigger feelings of low self-worth. And sometimes they're afraid even when there's no such person involved. Past confrontations with intimidators often leave scars.

Dealing with anger takes some of us back to scary childhood memories, perhaps to times when an adult's anger was dangerous. If these issues haven't been resolved, it's easy to fear any confrontation – even minor ones with reasonable people. And we don't want to face that fear. We'd rather run from it, as fast as our legs will carry us.

Sometimes we're afraid of confrontation because it means risking someone's disapproval. In some relationships, that can be hard to take. And sometimes we're afraid of our own reactions. Some people avoid confrontation because they believe that they'll lose their tempers and say things they'll regret. They're running away from the guilt and shame that often comes with such mistakes.

For some, confrontation means failure. If you're the peacemaker, the one who helps people to understand each other and get over their anger, you may see confrontation as a personal failure. Or you might be afraid of a different kind of failure: losing the battle itself. What if the person won't change? What if you can't get what you're entitled to? How will you feel then?

When your fear is in control, you always lose.

Any or all of these issues can lead us to fear confrontation. When your fear is in control, you always lose. As soon as you take charge, even in small ways, the balance of power changes and your life soon becomes your own. If you're intimidated by the very thought of an argument, I encourage you to explore your fears. Find out what you're so afraid of and decide how to deal with it. If the fear comes from abuse or any other kind of trauma, I encourage you to find a professional to help you get past it. You don't need to face this on your own.

Saying Yes to End the Conversation

How often have you been tempted to give in to something just to end the conversation? Have you ever wondered what gives that conversation its power – why you're willing to sacrifice so much to end it? Don't worry; I have good news for you. That power comes from **you** – specifically from your desire to avoid guilt, shame and other difficult emotions. Your fear of those feelings drives you to agree to things that don't work for you.

Manipulators know how to use tactics like rejection and disapproval to get what they want. These things don't feel good, and they're happy to use them repeatedly until you can't take any more. They know that when your emotional pain gets strong enough, you'll give them whatever they want. You've been a slave to your fear.

Why is this good news? Because you have the power to change. The next time you find yourself ready to give in to something, press the pause button. Stop talking, take a breath, and firmly state that you need some time to think. If you encounter resistance to this crazy idea, simply repeat it and walk away.

Once some time (and therefore the mental haze) has passed, consider what you almost agreed to. Does it feel right? Is it consistent with your values? Is it good for you and others? If it isn't, then think about your next steps. Decide how and when to set your boundary. If doing so in person seems too difficult, find another way. Send a text or an email, or call when you know the phone won't be answered and leave a message. Make it clear that you don't want to talk about it any further, and don't make yourself available for further discussion.

But what if you're not feeling guilty or ashamed? What if the other person won't take *no* for an answer, and you're too tired to keep resisting? Some people wear us down with their persistence (a polite word for their stubborn refusal to respect our boundaries).

The issue here is a bit different, although the solution is the same. You've simply forgotten your power. You have the right – and the ability – to end a conversation whenever it suits you. Unless the other person has authority over you, you don't need to answer her questions. Face your fear and take back your power. If you're feeling worn down, don't give in. Rather give yourself some rest by walking away. We'll look at this situation in more detail in Chapter 7, *Giving in to Pressure*.

There is one more aspect of this that I'd like to discuss. Some people give in because they find it difficult to say *no*. (The reasons for this were covered in Chapter 2, under the heading *No Is a Bad Word*.) Repeating it, or staying with it for a while, intensifies the discomfort. Saying *yes* provides an escape. Once again, the solution is the same. Insist on some time to think; get some distance from the situation. Then make your decision without the interference of those intense emotions and decide how to best communicate it.

It's called "your life" for a reason.

Saying Yes to Avoid Feeling Ashamed

Sometimes we agree to things because we're ashamed to admit the truth. You might be afraid of heights but agree to go skydiving with friends. Now you'll need a last-minute excuse to get out of it. Or you might agree to spend time with someone you dislike because you're ashamed of your feelings. Everyone else likes him, and you don't have a "logical" reason for feeling the way you do. When your friend suggests including him in your Friday afternoon cocktails, you don't know how to respond without giving yourself away. But is the truth so bad?

One of Steve's friends asks him to make a pledge for his walkathon. The money goes to a children's charity, and his friends have all signed up. Steve just moved to a new apartment, and the move cost him more than he expected. Money is tight for the next couple of months. He would love to say, "Not this time," but he's too ashamed to admit that he can't afford it. He pledges $20, wondering how he's going to come up with the money when his friend comes collecting next week. If Steve had explained the situation, his friend would have understood. And he would have saved himself the added financial pressure.

Unlike Steve's friend, some people are quite happy to shame us into doing what they want. When we don't agree to their demands, they'll tell us how selfish or stupid we are, or how much pain we're causing others:

"If you're too blind to see how much your brother needs you," (in other words, you're stupid), "then I guess the whole family will suffer." (You're the cause of our pain.)

"I thought I raised you to be more supportive." (You're selfish and you're letting me down.)

Giving people what they want may stop the shame for the moment, but we end up feeling even worse later. Besides feeling selfish or foolish, we're ashamed of ourselves for being bullied. No one enjoys feeling like a victim.

Imagining the Worst

Imagining the worst is another way we give in to our fears. We do things that aren't right for us to keep our jobs, avoid rejection or "keep the peace." But often our fears are unfounded. When you're feeling threatened, try asking yourself these questions:

Is what I'm afraid of likely to happen?
Is it really so hard to deal with?
What other options do I have?

Since Joanne's father died, her mother has been lonely. Joanne calls her every evening after dinner, asking about her day and telling her what the kids are up to. She also brings her to dinner every Sunday for a change of scenery and a chance to be with her grandchildren. Lately she's been under pressure at the office, and when dinner is finished, she still has work to do. She finds talking to her mother stressful, as she's worried about falling behind.

Tonight she doesn't want to call. But she knows her mother will be hurt if she doesn't. She doesn't have many friends at the nursing home, and she needs the company. If she doesn't call, her mother will think that she doesn't care, that spending time with her is a burden. She can't stand the thought of her mother feeling alone and unloved.

As you may have noticed, Joanne has filled her head with the worst possible outcome. Let's go through the questions one at a time and see what happens:

Is her mother likely to react this way? This question is important because we tend to throw logic to the wind once we get caught up in fear. We must look at all the possibilities, not just the unpleasant ones, and assess the likelihood of a serious problem. Sometimes our imaginations get the best of us and we end up believing that we'll lose our jobs if we can't make it to the end-of-year party.

Joanne's mother has always been an understanding person, willing to accommodate others' needs. Unless Joanne cuts her off without explanation, she is unlikely to complain – or conclude that her daughter has suddenly stopped loving her.

Would that be so hard to deal with? This question prevents us from letting our fear blow things out of proportion. Sometimes we forget that we do know how to cope with life's challenges.

In the unlikely event that her mother becomes unreasonable, Joanne can still manage. She may feel guilty, but if she handles the situation properly it will work itself out (in other words, her mother will get over it).

What other options does she have? This is my favorite question, because answering it may allow us to prevent the problem from happening in the first place.

Joanne could get her work done first and call her mother later in the evening. That would take the stress away and give her an easy way to talk about the extra work. She could then work out a new arrangement with her mother until the pressure is off. She could call less often during the week, and wait until she finishes her work. Her mother could make another arrangement when she knows her daughter isn't calling. She might call a friend or another relative, or she could spend more time chatting with people at dinner.

Joanne's fear led her to expect a rigid and self-centered response from her mother, which is not her way. Asking herself a few simple questions would make it clear that she can get what she needs without hurting her mother.

Starting Down the Slippery Slope

Maureen's sister asked her to help plan her husband's 30th birthday celebration. Maureen agreed. They set aside a few hours the following weekend to get ideas at the local party store. "Thanks for helping me," her sister said. "Two heads are so much better than one!"

When her sister needed to work on Saturday morning, she asked Maureen to go without her. Maureen dutifully went by herself, writing down ideas as she walked through the store. She then emailed them to her sister.

The following weekend was invitation time. Maureen's sister asked her to come by on Saturday morning to address the invitations with her. But, just like last weekend, she needed to work. She asked Maureen to start without her, promising to be back before 11:00. But rather than coming home right away, she did her grocery shopping and other errands, leaving Maureen to finish the job herself.

When the time came, her sister made a few phone calls and rented a tent for the backyard. She wanted her husband to be surprised, so she took him out in the morning while Maureen set up everything. (Of course, her husband had plenty of golf buddies who would have been happy to keep him occupied.) And when the party was over, she disappeared with him, leaving Maureen to supervise the dismantling of the tent. Some family and friends stayed to help clean up, so at least she made it home before dinner time. What a relief!

Looking back on the whole thing, Maureen felt used. Her sister had done this to her before and would no doubt do it again.

So how did this happen? And how will Maureen deal with her growing resentment toward her sister?

Maureen had several opportunities to set limits. When her sister asked her to go to the party store alone, Maureen let her know through her tone of voice that she was "none too pleased" – but she went anyway. She could have insisted that they reschedule, reminding her sister that "two heads are better than one".

When her sister wasn't available to address her own invitations, Maureen had several choices: rescheduling (perhaps at her own home), bringing her share home and dropping them off at the end of the weekend, or telling her sister that she was also busy.

Are you getting the picture? At each stage, Maureen agreed to go further down that slippery slope. Certainly she was pushed ... but she never pushed back. Why? Because she was afraid of her emotions.

She didn't want to confront her sister; she knew that she'd have her excuses lined up. She also knew (or at least thought she knew) how it would all end: "If you don't want to help, just say so!" And then she'd feel so guilty!

Don't let someone else's problems become your own.

If you're anything like Maureen, you'll need to think carefully about what you agree to. You may need to take some extra time for your decision, so that you can understand when you truly want to help and when you're running from your emotional pain. If you're prepared to help, you'll need to make sure the parameters are clear: Exactly what does "plan a party" mean? Be clear about what you're willing to do – and where your limits are – from the beginning. Consider expressing your *no* right along with your *yes*:

I'll be happy to help you come up with a to-do list, but that's all I have time for this weekend.

I can meet you at the store and spend up to two hours with you, but then I have to leave.

Call me when you're ready to start the invitations and I'll join you.

When that slope gets steep and the expectations suddenly increase, don't let someone else's problems become your own. Refuse to be pressured; take a few deep breaths and think about yourself before responding. If you need to check your schedule, say so. If you don't feel comfortable and you don't know why, consider saying that. Give a timeframe for your response and stick to it.

We slide down the slippery slope because we allow our emotions to make our decisions for us. We want to be liked. We identify with the panic in someone's voice. Thinking that someone needs us makes us feel important; seeing ourselves as selfish makes us feel ashamed. But when we allow these feelings to rule us, we end up feeling angry and resentful. Make "I think before I commit!" your new mantra. It will serve you well.

Getting Sucked into Someone Else's Drama

Kyra's best friend is always in crisis. If it isn't a problem with her latest boyfriend, it's someone in her social circle or her "ridiculously demanding" boss. Kyra feels sorry for her friend and often spends hours listening to her troubles and giving her advice. But it seems there's always a reason why her suggestions won't work, and she doesn't know how to end these unpleasant conversations.

Kyra feels others' pain too intensely. She makes their problems her own because she won't feel better until they're solved. What she doesn't realize is that no one can solve someone else's problems. We all need to face our own challenges. Others can give us advice, but their ideas come from their own beliefs and values. They may not work for us.

Kyra also needs to understand that her friend doesn't want solutions. All she wants is attention, which her "suffering" is designed to obtain. It's not that her friend consciously creates problems. It's just that at some level she's learned that when people pay attention to her, she feels better. And she's found people who will pay attention when she has a problem. Kyra is one of those people.

Kyra sees herself as altruistic, but is she? Not really. Her behavior is based on self-interest. She works hard to solve her friend's problems because she feels her friend's pain. And she won't feel better until she finds a solution. This gives her friend too much power. She can reject solutions indefinitely. Because no solution is good enough, Kyra stays uncomfortable.

Can you relate? If so, it's important that you learn to let go of others' wants and needs long enough to focus on your own.

To accomplish this, you'll need to take a good look at yourself, beginning with your thoughts and feelings in the moment. How do you feel when someone relies on you? Do you have a sense of responsibility? Does the opportunity to help someone temporarily lift your spirits? Do you like being needed, or do you feel obligated to help? What's happening within you?

If you're dealing with others' problems at the expense of your own, then something matters more to you than living your own life. Find out what it is. Make a commitment to changing these patterns and taking your life back. Learn to accept that your needy friend will suffer whether you talk for two hours or 20 minutes (or not at all). See her challenges as growth opportunities rather than crises. Face your fear of being unimportant. (This is a big one for many of us.) These things take time and commitment, but the freedom they bring is more than worth the price.

Focusing on What You Want to Avoid

Everyone wants to avoid pain; we're hardwired for that. This will not change – nor should it. The problem starts when we focus too much on what we want to avoid. You see, we tend to attract more of whatever we focus on. This may not seem logical at first, but it's the truth. Let's look at an example.

Do you remember Joanne? She grew up with an angry, alcoholic father and an enabling mother. All she wants is harmony; she's only happy when everyone around her is happy. She has a knack for anticipating people's needs – and going out of her way to provide for them. Her friends have come to expect her advice, her baby-sitting services and even her cooking whenever they feel a bit overwhelmed. Joanne is always there with a smile, an encouraging word – and a casserole, if she thinks that will help. Just don't ask for her opinion on anything controversial!

Joanne hasn't argued with anyone in years (except, of course, with her teenagers). On the surface, her life appears remarkably peaceful. But appearances can be deceiving.

Although she works hard not to show it, Joanne is on edge most of the time. Because of her history, she's sensitive to any sign of potential conflict. This means she's often busy worrying about problems that don't even exist – except in her mind. And she's too busy dealing with everyone else to make time for herself.

On top of that, Joanne doesn't feel deeply connected to her friends or family. That's because she's never able to be herself with them – or allow them to be themselves if that involves the risk of conflict. Although everyone knows she'll be there for them, Joanne's real feelings are a mystery. She does her best to agree with everyone – and changes the subject when she (or they) can't agree. The truth is that she often feels unsupported, and she wishes she could relax and let her guard down once in a while.

Avoiding conflict has not given Joanne a happy, fulfilling or even peaceful life.

You see, conflict isn't the real issue. In fact, there's nothing inherently wrong with it. Joanne doesn't avoid it because it's wrong or dangerous. She avoids it because it terrifies her. It's not the conflict she's avoiding – it's her fear.

Your fear of conflict will keep you from experiencing real peace.

Once you understand that Joanne is running from fear rather than conflict, the problem becomes clear. Reacting to even the subtlest cues means that she sees the potential for conflict everywhere. This triggers more fear, which is exactly what she was trying to avoid.

You may be able to avoid external conflict. But your fear of it will prevent you from experiencing the peace you seek.

We run from so many things: conflict, rejection, disapproval, blame, criticism, even failure. But there's nothing wrong with any of them. What we're really running from is the feelings they trigger. We're afraid of our most painful emotions, and we'll do almost anything to avoid them. Anything but face them, that is.

And that's the key. Our emotions won't go anywhere until we face them. We can't run from them; they're attached to us. We can suppress them at times, but they'll just resurface – often with a vengeance.

Emotional freedom doesn't mean that you don't experience any pain. It means that you're not a slave to that pain. You're not so afraid of it that you'll turn tail and run whenever it rises to the surface. You can face it, even though you don't want to, and move on. Once you do that, you stop living in the past. You stop being unable to enjoy the present for fear that the future might hurt. And you're finally able to enjoy the peace that you wanted all along.

Feeling Not Good Enough

Low self-esteem – the belief that we're not good enough – can be one of the most painful feelings in the world. It's also one that appears to defy logic, as it can affect everyone from movie stars and successful entrepreneurs to a man who's just lost his job. Our self-image is formed when we're young, based on feedback from parents and others close to us. Material success – or failure – seems to have little effect on it.

People with low self-esteem may trust the opinions of others more than their own instincts; this may be why Maureen stayed at that party when she'd rather be home watching TV. Like Joanne, they may blindly follow the rules of their societies, religions or family and friends without stopping to consider their own values and beliefs. They may see others as more important or believe that they can't manage without their support.

When we don't value ourselves, we look to others for approval. And often we'll do whatever it takes to avoid disapproval, rejection and the emotional pain that comes with them. When we don't feel good enough, we lack the confidence to set good boundaries. And when we finally do say *no*, we're likely to make excuses for it – and allow others to manipulate us into a *yes*.

For these reasons, low self-esteem can make it extremely difficult, even painful, to say *no*. If you suspect that this is the reason you're struggling, I urge you to get the help you need.

Running Away

When we run from our pain, we bear the cost. We stop living according to our highest values, which is the only true source of fulfillment. We sacrifice our own priorities for someone else's. We live a quiet lie. And then we discover the awful truth: Running doesn't protect us from the pain. It perpetuates it.

At the end of the day, it all comes down to fear and shame. Anger and conflict may take us back to a childhood when anger easily turned into rage. Disapproval may have led to beatings. Rejection (or a lack of love and affection) can lead us to believe that we aren't good enough. We feel ashamed of who we are.

Facing these feelings is hard. But it's worth doing, because running away hurts even more. Instead of confronting our pain, we do whatever it takes to avoid it – which usually makes us feel even worse.

One of the most common strategies for avoiding this pain is people-pleasing. As we'll see in the next chapter, this is often a form of manipulation. I know that sounds strange, but it's true. We engage in people-pleasing to get something (usually approval) from someone who might not give it to us otherwise. Keep reading to find out why approval is so important to us – and why people-pleasing can never give us what we're longing for.

5TH CHAPTER

LOOKING FOR APPROVAL?

As we've seen in the last chapter, fear is a powerful motivator. For some, the need to please others is just as strong. These emotions can be so intense that they override our values. We do things that we wouldn't otherwise do.

The "disease to please" (a phrase made popular by the late Harriet B Braiker) runs some people's lives. When we don't feel good about ourselves, we rely on others for temporary relief. When someone is pleased with something we've said or done, we feel good for a little while. Our feelings of low self-esteem give way to the possibility that we're not so bad after all.

Psychologists call this *external validation*. We all benefit from getting some now and then, but relying on it is a recipe for victimhood. The more you need the approval of others, the more power they have over you. And when you compromise your values in exchange for someone's approval, you reinforce all your negative beliefs about yourself. The approval is short-lived, but the self-judgment endures. You feel even worse than before. It's a vicious circle.

Looking for Agreement

Many people who feel controlled by others are in that position because they want their agreement. They want someone to confirm that they're right – that their boundaries are not just reasonable, but necessary. So they come up with all kinds of ways to justify their decisions. But instead of agreement, all they get is an endless debate.

Sometimes we need agreement. Business partners must agree on their strategies and budgets. Couples must agree on how to raise their children. And when you need to say *no* to a good friend, you'd like her to understand your reasons. You want her to know you care. But when we look for agreement from everyone, we can easily end up tired and resentful.

Before you start explaining your decisions, ask yourself some questions. Why do you value this person's opinion? Is it because you're in unfamiliar territory – for example, you have no experience with legal issues and this person deals with them every day? Or do you feel better when others put their stamp of approval on your opinions and choices? If you're looking for information, get whatever you need. But if you're looking for someone to say that you're right, chances are you're giving away your power.

Do you remember Linda, the one whose brother is out of work? Her mother is still pressuring her to take him in. Linda has been on the phone all weekend, gathering support for her position. Having convinced her friends that refusing is the only reasonable choice, she's now working on her father.

Dad, has Mom told you about her latest scheme? She wants me to let Danny stay in my spare room until he finds a job! Can you believe that?

Her father doesn't say a word.

I mean, Dad, how can I have a life of my own with my lazy brother hanging around all the time? He's not my responsibility – and God knows how long it will take him to find a job this time. And then he still has to save up for the deposits. It's just not fair!

Her father is silent.

Admit it, Dad. You know I'm right.

Her father finally speaks. "Honey, you know that whatever you decide, you'll still be my one and only little girl."

Linda is furious. She isn't looking for a declaration of fatherly love. She wants to hear her father say that she's absolutely right – her mother's demands are beyond reason. She wants him to agree with her that laziness is the only reason Danny can't keep a job. She wants him to tell her that he completely understands and supports her decision. No one should expect her to give up her life for her lazy brother. And, of course, she wants him to tell all of this to her mother as well.

But that's not going to happen.

Linda believes that she needs her father to agree with her. Why? Because she's feeling guilty. She knows that her parents moved to an apartment when her father was laid off from the bank. There isn't much room for Danny there. He and his father don't get along well, either, so things will be tense. That's why her mother is pushing her to take Danny in.

Linda has a tough decision to make. At the end of the day, it doesn't matter who agrees with her and who doesn't. Her father says he loves her regardless, and her mother's attempts to pressure her are irrelevant. What matters is that she's comfortable with her own decision. She will only feel good about herself when she makes the decision that's right for her, considering her feelings about living with her brother and her concern for the rest of her family. No one can do that for her.

Kyra is facing a different dilemma. Her last relationship ended badly, and she wants to spend some time alone. It's the weekend, and her friends are trying to cheer her up. They've decided to spend Saturday night at a comedy club. Kyra knows what she wants, but she's having a tough time convincing her friends.

Thank you for trying to look after me. But all I really want is to spend some quiet time at home. I don't feel like going out yet.

"Come on. Kyra, it's no good moping around at home. This is just the kind of distraction you need. A good laugh will make you forget he ever existed!"

Thanks, but ...

"Kyra, you know we're right. You said the same thing last time, but getting out got your mind off things."

Yes, but ...

"We won't take *no* for an answer. I'll pick you up at 6:30."

Alright ... (sighing).

Kyra knows what she wants. But she's so used to pleasing everyone else that she doesn't know how to communicate the importance of her own needs. She wants everyone to be happy.

If Kyra were willing to risk disagreement, here's how the conversation might have gone:

Thank you for trying to look after me. But all I really want is to spend some quiet time at home. I don't feel like going out yet.

"Come on. Kyra, it's no good moping around at home. This is just the kind of distraction you need. A good laugh will make you forget he ever existed!"

I'm just not ready for that. Right now I need some quiet time. I feel sad, and I've spent the whole week at work pretending everything's fine. I need time to cry, and maybe even to think about my life. I have to do this alone.

"You're missing out on a great time...."

I know. And I'd love to go out and have some fun once I've had my thinking time. I'm lucky to have such great friends. Thanks for understanding.

Here Kyra explains why she needs to be alone. Rather than giving in so that everyone can agree, she shares how she feels and what she needs. This gives her friends the opportunity to understand and respect her decision.

Sometimes our search for agreement is less obvious. When self-doubt takes over, we may not even want to express our opinions. Remember Joanne, who's been running away from conflict all these years? She never offers her opinion first. She waits to see what others think so there's no risk of conflict. She keeps away from controversial topics like politics and religion, and she makes sure she's covered when it comes to everything else.

Here's a typical lunchtime conversation with Joanne and her co-workers:

"What do you think of the new boss? Is he pushy or what?"

Joanne looks around the table, seeing several nods and grimaces. She hopes the subject will change soon.

"Yes, he is. Maybe he'll relax a bit once he's used to us."

"Oh, I doubt it. Guys like that don't change."

"Just give him a chance. Time will tell."

"What do you think, Joanne?"

Joanne's heart skips a beat. She likes the new guy. He's confident, and he seems to know what he's doing. She's hoping the department will finally run smoothly now that there's a competent manager. Still, she doesn't want to rock the boat.

Me? Oh … I don't know.

"Sure you do! You've worked with him more than any of us. What do you think?"

Thinking quickly, she replies, "He is a little pushy. But he seems to have a lot of experience; maybe we'll be better off in the end. Aren't we all tired of rushing around at the last minute because the boss forgot another deadline?"

"You think he cares about us? A selfish jerk like that?"

Joanne turns pale. "No … of course not … I'm just hoping he can do a better job. I don't know. That's what I hope. I guess time will tell."

As you can see, Joanne chooses her words to minimize conflict. She says that the new boss is pushy, even though she doesn't think so. She makes a tentative statement about his experience, but she backs off at the first sign of disagreement, relying on someone else's words ("time will tell") to smooth things over. She goes along with statements that he's selfish and uncaring, even though she doesn't believe that.

If you need others to agree with your choices, you aren't trusting yourself.

If you find yourself acting like Joanne, know that you're not alone. We all prefer agreement to disagreement. It's just a matter of how much we want that agreement and what we're willing to do for it. But we're all individuals with our own beliefs, values and backgrounds. We're not supposed to agree on everything – even when it really matters to us.

If you're ready to kick the agreement addiction, you can start by expressing your honest opinion more often and making small decisions without consulting others. Do what feels right to you and notice how it works out. When you like the results, congratulate yourself. If things don't work out the way you'd like, learn from the experience. Why didn't your choice work for you? How did you feel when someone challenged your opinion? Do you need some help in dealing with those feelings, or is it a matter of time and practice?

If you need others to agree with your choices, you aren't trusting yourself. Others may have strong opinions, but what's true for them may not be true for you. No one shares all your values, beliefs and life experiences. So learn to trust yourself. You'll enjoy your life a lot more when you do.

Compromising Yourself and Your Values for Approval

When I asked Google for the definition of *approval*, this is what I found:

1. The action of officially agreeing to something or accepting something as satisfactory.
2. The belief that someone or something is good or acceptable.

Agreement is about an opinion or a decision. You and your spouse can agree (or disagree) on the best schools for your children. The approval that we seek is much more than that. We want others to think highly of us, to see us as "good," "acceptable" or "satisfactory."

At some point, we've all needed someone else's approval. As children, we need others to show us that we're good enough just the way we are. And of course, we look to our parents and other authority figures for that validation. Children who consistently receive love and support, and are able to meet the challenges life brings them, grow into confident adults. Those who don't receive enough love, or the support they need to cope with adversity, may face a life of self-doubt. (Children who are protected from life's challenges may also come to doubt themselves. When that protection ends, they may be unable to handle things that others take in stride.)

Doubting yourself is painful. Do it for long enough and you'll become an easy target for manipulators. When they express their disapproval (which they will do whenever you put your wants and needs before theirs), you'll feel terrible about yourself. And you'll desperately want those feelings to stop. As soon as you gain their approval (which you can easily do by putting them first), you'll heave a sigh of relief as those awful feelings melt away.

Laura got married when she was only 19. Looking back, she realizes that she accepted the proposal because she thought she couldn't do any better. Her friends and family were against it, but she didn't listen. She thought this was her only chance at happiness.

As soon as they were married, her husband started controlling her. Laura did everything he wanted. She changed the way she dressed because she was "attracting too much attention from dangerous men." She stopped her studies because starting a family was more important. (Laura wanted children, but only when she was in her thirties.) And she stopped seeing her friends because they could only socialize with other couples. After all, they were married now. Naturally some things would change.

Laura agreed to all of this and more to stop the pain she felt when she went against her husband's wishes. The guilt and shame were simply too much for her. She couldn't stand the thought of being a bad wife.

So why, she wondered, wasn't the sacrifice paying off? Why did she feel even worse than she had before she got married? And why did her husband leave her after a couple of years? Being a good person should have made her feel better. And being a good wife should have kept her married. What went wrong? And why, nearly 10 years later, was she still unable to have a good relationship with a man?

Giving in to the demands of others, especially those close to us, seems like a great idea in the moment. It makes those awful feelings disappear. But where do they go – and what are they replaced with?

That sense of unworthiness doesn't go away when you do someone else's bidding. If it did, once would be enough; you wouldn't need to run from it again. But that's not how it works. The relief is only temporary. The shame is still there, just under the surface, waiting for the next trigger. And the more you sacrifice, the more you sell yourself short to keep others happy, the worse you feel. Whether you acknowledge it or not, you resent their demands. You feel angry with yourself for succumbing to them. The whole experience leaves you feeling stupid, weak and powerless.

Giving in doesn't seem like such a great idea after all.

Laura won't feel any better until she does what's right for her, whether the men in her life like it or not. She has traded some of her highest values for men who expect her to live without them. Until she stops doing their bidding, she will continue to suffer.

Worrying about Other People's Judgments

Sometimes we do things "for others" without their direct involvement. Even when there's no one standing in front of us expressing their disapproval, we may still do things that don't work for us because we're afraid of what people might think. *How will it look? What will people say?* Basing our decisions on the answers to these questions leads to an empty life.

What other people think of you
is none of your business!

A wise teacher once told me, "What other people think of you is none of your business." I agree. Other people's opinions are based on **their** values, **their** beliefs and **their** life experiences. They may provide you with some useful input, but your choices must be based on your own values, beliefs and experiences. This is the secret to a happy and fulfilling life.

Living according to someone else's rules is more common than you might think. Even when we're not worried about anyone in particular ("What would my mother think?"), we're still under the influence of society. As children, we took in the beliefs and values of our culture. Our families, our teachers and our peers made us what we are today. Our brains developed through our interactions with them – and, of course, through the hours spent in front of the TV, at the movie theater or immersed in books and magazines. The media influences us more than we'd like to believe.

Our environment shaped and molded us as we grew; our experiences, and how we responded to them, defined us. We are who we are because of others. But that doesn't mean we can't learn to make our own choices now.

What if you're a woman contemplating the importance of career and family? If you come from a conservative background, your family and friends may assume that your career will end with the arrival of your first child. If you're well educated, those close to you might assume that your career will continue – or that you'll wait to have children. If both are true, you may find the people close to you pulling you in opposite directions.

It's often easiest to fall in line with your culture (or the part of it that you're most identified with). But that will only bring you happiness if it's in alignment with your core values and beliefs. If you want a fulfilling life, you'll need to make the choices that are best for you. That means knowing not only your values and beliefs, but your personality. Are you the kind of person who would enjoy full-time parenthood, or do you need more mental stimulation? How important is that money to you and your family? Will you cry every morning when leave your child at daycare, or will you see it as a worthwhile sacrifice?

Before making any major decision, I encourage you to consider these kinds of issues. We often consider practical matters in some detail and stop there. Contemplating your values with respect to an upcoming decision is a good way to get to know yourself better. It will also help you to feel good about your decisions. If you think that those close to you will judge you harshly, understanding where you differ will help you to stand your ground.

Most of your beliefs were given to you by others, so question them from time to time. Make sure they work for you. Being happy is about living according to your highest values. Make sure they're really yours.

Buying into Other People's Judgments
There's something you must remember about other people's judgments: they belong to other people. What they think can't hurt us, unless we internalize it. In other words, no one else's opinion can affect how you feel about yourself ... unless you already suspect that it's true.

Let's check in on Laura, who has that habit of attracting the wrong men. You might remember that she gave up her studies to have a family with her ex-husband, who dumped her anyway. Laura wants to go back to school, but she's worried about what her friends and family will think. She's tested the waters with a few close friends, all of whom have been supportive. She's decided it's time to approach her mother.

"Are you out of your mind?!" she cries. "You've got a good job, and you're finally starting to save some money. Why risk all of that on some pie in the sky nonsense? You have everything you need. Why aren't you ever satisfied?"

Laura goes pale. What was she thinking? She makes enough to pay the bills, to save up for a nice vacation every couple of years – she's even started a retirement plan. The work might be a bit boring, but she's made friends at the office. And what if she failed? What if her grades weren't good enough? What if she screwed up the interviews? Maybe her mother was right. Why rock the boat?

Laura's mother gave up her own dreams decades ago, when she became a single mom. Over the years she convinced herself that she couldn't do any better and that "good enough is good enough". That's how she coped. And she won't let anyone prove her wrong.

By calling her dreams "pie in the sky nonsense," she tells her daughter that she doesn't believe in her – and that she's wrong to want more from life. And instead of believing in herself, Laura buys into her mother's fears.

The problem isn't that Laura's mother doesn't believe in her dreams. The problem is that she doesn't believe in herself.

Wanting to Belong

Belong is such an interesting word. It refers to ownership: "The rights to that music belong to me," or being part of something: "He belongs to our church." But it also refers to being well suited: "They belong with each other." There's a big difference between "belonging to" and "belonging with." We confuse these concepts all the time, singing "You belong to me," in our love songs.

In evolutionary terms, being part of a group increased our chances of survival. This is especially true for women, who needed to protect their children as well as themselves. Scientists now believe that our brains evolved to meet the challenge of complex group dynamics. It seems we're wired to be part of a group.

Connecting with others relieves stress; warm interactions calm the amygdala's fight-or-flight response. And if you're feeling lonely, a group of like-minded people can be the perfect cure.

Although the act of connection is important, whom we connect with is even more important. Spending time with people who don't fully respect us, or who bring us down in other ways, defeats the purpose. Belonging is about common interests and shared values:

"Birds of a feather flock together." If we stay with a group that isn't right for us, we lose the benefits of true connection. We don't *belong* with them, so there's no lasting benefit.

When you become part of a group,
make sure you get what you came for.

Authentic relationships, based on trust and respect, make us feel emotionally safe. They give meaning to our lives. That's what we're searching for when we want to belong. So, when we become part of a group, it's important to make sure that we're getting what we came for.

Remember Joe, whose boss wanted to know how the new guy was working out? Joe so wanted to be "one of the boys" that he overlooked his new friend's behavior – and the problems it would cause for him and his co-workers. When the boss asked him for an evaluation, he didn't know what to do. He didn't want to stop feeling like "one of the boys".

But if telling the truth means that his new group rejects him, then those connections aren't worth much. As hard as that might be to face, Joe would be better off looking for other places to connect. He won't feel good about himself if he lies to the boss; his relationship with the group would do him more harm than good.

Are you worried that doing the right thing will jeopardize your status as part of a group? Does spending time with them leave you feeling worse instead of better? If so, it might be time to look for a group that's more suited to you – one where you'll be both accepted and respected. If you can't find one right away, work on accepting and respecting yourself. There's no substitute for that.

Fear of Rejection

Although many people crave approval, others are driven by a subtler force: fear of rejection. Rather than looking for signs that they're OK, they're afraid of losing what they have.

Steve has a friend who looked after him in school. He still appreciates Mike's guidance and protection; he would do anything for him. And Mike knows it.

In the past year, Mike has developed a drinking problem. Steve has driven him home from too many bars and helped him through too many hangovers. Steve knows that enabling Mike to continue his binges isn't helping him. But he's afraid of losing his friendship. Being rejected by someone who has played such an important role in his life seems like too much to bear.

Just like those who crave approval, Steve fears rejection because he doesn't feel secure about himself. Mike's friendship and the good feelings that come with it are important to him. But remember what we learned about other people's judgments: they belong to others. What you don't already believe at some level cannot affect your self-esteem. If Mike rejects his friend for no longer enabling his destructive behavior, that says plenty about Mike – and nothing about Steve. Steve won't buy into the idea that he's not a good friend unless he's already doubting himself. If he can't handle Mike's reaction, the real problem is Steve's relationship with himself.

At the same time, we are social creatures. Steve may need to rely on his other friends to get through this. But if he acts according to his highest values, and he has friends who respect those values, he should feel good about his choices and have all the support he needs. Even one good friend is enough. With a little help, Steve should be able to do what he knows is right.

Approval and Manipulation: Who Do You Want to Be?

Successful manipulation is almost always a two-way street. The only clear exception to this is lying. When people lie, you may base important decisions on those lies. You're acting on what you believe to be true, and that's that. But other situations are not so simple.

When we give others what they want in order to get their approval, aren't we're trying to control them?

When we're looking for approval, it's easier for others to control us. We call the people who are willing to do this *manipulators*. But in doing so, we ignore our own role in the interaction. When we give others what they want in order to get their approval, aren't we trying to control them? Isn't that also manipulative?

This isn't just an ethical issue. The problem with giving others what they want is that, while it may offer temporary relief, we end up destroying the very self-worth we were trying to protect. Consider Laura, who keeps falling for the wrong men. She relates to them through a façade, designed to attract their attention and ensure a continuous supply of flattery and flowers. She becomes someone else in order to make them happy, but it's never enough. She ends up more miserable than ever – even before they leave.

And then there's Joanne, who wants approval so much that she's afraid to express her own opinion. The cost of this hoped-for approval is her ability to be authentic. Joanne has no close relationships, because she's afraid to let anyone see her as she truly is. She's sacrificed any chance of real friendship for the temporary approval of people who hardly know her.

Even Sam, whose father wants him to take over his business someday, is engaged in a bit of manipulation. He wants his father's approval so much that he's never told him about the career he wants. The manipulation may not be conscious, but it's there. By withholding the truth, he avoids his father's disapproval. But how long can he pretend? And how successful can he be doing work that he doesn't enjoy?

Living Your Own Life

Approval is all about other people's beliefs and opinions. When we need external validation, it's because we aren't confident in ourselves. We don't believe we're smart enough, capable enough or good enough. We look for others' opinions because we don't trust our own. Their approval is a cheap substitute for self-respect. But a substitute won't do the job.

If you need the approval of others to feel good about yourself, it's time to take back your power. Earn the respect you're so desperately craving by living according to your own highest values rather than always pleasing others. And when people withhold their approval to get their way, take a deep breath and say to yourself, "That's OK. I'll never make everyone happy. And I don't need to," or, "The people who matter will still like me." (The ones who still like you when you do what's right for you **are** the ones who matter.) Or you could try my personal favorite: "They don't approve of my decision. But that's OK; I know what's right for me."

And what about all those people whose approval you're no longer seeking? Most of them will be just fine. Once they get over the shock, everything will go back to normal – except that you'll be doing what feels right to **you** now. As for the rest of them, the ones who won't accept the new you: What kind of people do you want in your life?

For some of us, other people's opinions aren't the issue. Sure, we'd like them to be happy with us. But even when those close to us are telling us we're fine, the voices in our heads tell a different story. When someone asks for our help – even when the request is unreasonable – we may feel to guilty to say *no*. In the next chapter, we'll explore the seven guilt traps and learn the best ways to escape them.

6TH CHAPTER

STUCK IN THE GULT TRAP?

Who isn't familiar with the dreaded guilt trip? Lines like these can immobilize us, causing us to give up on even the most reasonable boundaries:

"Don't you care what happens to me?"

"You know I can't manage without you."

"I guess family isn't important to you."

"I can always ask your sister. She's never too busy for me...."

"I thought we were friends!"

"You owe me."

"How can you be so selfish?"

Every one of these sentences has been carefully designed to make someone feel guilty. And, as we know from the chapter on emotional pain, some of us will do just about anything to avoid that feeling.

So how do you maintain reasonable boundaries with people who are willing to use guilt against you? The key is to understand what's happening in the interaction as well as what's right for you. Once you see things more clearly, you'll be able to make better choices. Let's look at some of the ways we succumb to guilt and what would change if we knew – and applied – the truth.

Doing Something Because You Feel Obligated

Joanne's aunt Theresa always encouraged her when she was young. She could go to her with any problem, knowing that she would feel better once they talked. Her aunt was single, and she liked to think of Joanne as her daughter. She often refers to herself as Joanne's "other mother".

Now that she's older, Theresa is getting lonely. Her closest friends have died, and she doesn't get out much. Family members have encouraged her to join clubs, visit the senior center, and make new friends. But she doesn't want to do those things, and she expects her family to be there for her.

Every Friday for the past month, Theresa has invited her niece to join her for lunch on Saturday. Joanne spends Saturday mornings driving her kids around; after that she still needs to make lunch and run errands. By the time she's finished, it's almost time for dinner. Every week the conversation ended the same way:

"Can't you afford a little time for your other mother? You know you're the closest thing I have to a daughter."

I'm sorry, but I can't. You know the kids have practice and Bill is working.

And every time Joanne hung up the phone and cried. *Why is life so unfair? Why must I keep saying* no *to someone who's been so good to me?*

Joanne is suffering for two reasons. First of all, she feels guilty because she doesn't pay much attention to her aunt. She's busy raising a family and working full-time, and she forgets Theresa until she calls with an impossible request. Part of her pain comes from feeling selfish and ungrateful.

Secondly, her aunt intensifies these feelings by playing the "other mother" card. With this simple phrase, she brings up all of Joanne's feelings of obligation and guilt. If it weren't for the children, she would give Theresa whatever she wanted.

These words have created an artificial link between Theresa's weekly invitation and her niece's sense of obligation. Because she has never questioned that link, Joanne feels guilty every time she says *no* to lunch. She feels sorry for Theresa's loneliness and sees herself as a bad person for not doing something about it. And since she can't do what's been asked of her, she feels helpless as well: *Why is life so unfair?*

Once Joanne separates her gratitude to her aunt from Saturday's lunch, a few things will happen. First, the unhealthy guilt will subside; she won't need to cry every week because she can't make it to lunch. Next, she can look at her relationship with her aunt and explore where her choices have matched her values and where they haven't. Now that she's looking at things consciously, she's no longer powerless. Joanne can decide for herself how she would like to repay her aunt's kindness.

She might decide to call her once a week and chat for a while – maybe set aside a regular time for the call. And there are some relatives who live closer to her. Perhaps someone would be willing to bring her out once a month to spend time with the family. Theresa loves children; maybe they could invite her to come for Sunday lunch.

In this case, some of the guilt that Joanne has been feeling makes sense. Her lack of attention to her aunt violated her own values: she was neglecting someone special to her. Once she starts paying more attention to her, she'll feel better about herself. The guilt will subside.

All of this becomes possible once she breaks that artificial link and considers what **she** wants to do for Theresa. If you feel obligated to someone, it's up to you to decide how to meet that obligation. How to repay kindness is a choice that no one can make for you. After all, a gift isn't a gift if the giver decides how you reciprocate. That's a business transaction.

Accepting Unwanted Gifts or Favors

Accepting gifts and favors is the perfect way to make yourself feel obligated. If you've asked for the favor, or if the gift is part of a balanced relationship, no problem. When that's not the case, it pays to think carefully before accepting it.

The classic example of this is, of course, a man buying expensive jewelry for a woman. She knows that accepting it creates an expectation. It's safe to assume that any gift or favor coming from someone we don't know very well comes with expectations – even if it's only the hope of spending more time together. After all, we don't generally do nice things for people who don't interest us.

Consider the consequences of accepting a favor.

I'm not suggesting that all unexpected favors should be refused – not at all. But it pays to consider the consequences of accepting them. Take the time to question any gift that seems inappropriate for the nature of the relationship. Become clear about what you feel comfortable accepting and what you don't. Ask yourself what the consequences are likely to be – both of accepting and of declining. And if you're part of a couple making such a decision, take the time to understand each other's perspectives and come to an agreement.

The biggest problem for couples seems to be gifts from in-laws. Parents may give lavish gifts or gifts that make decisions for you – like furniture, pets or vacations with them. Spouses often disagree on whether to accept these gifts. This can be quite a challenge, but handled properly it can make your relationship stronger.

Years ago, a colleague of mine received furniture from her wealthy father. He had it shipped from India before he came to the US to visit. It was beautiful – the kind of thing she loved but they could not afford. She accepted the gift, but her husband was **not** happy. I can understand his feelings. His father-in-law chose what their living room would look like without consulting either of them. He knew that his gift would be difficult to refuse; it certainly couldn't be returned for a refund! I don't know how (or whether) they resolved the issue. I only hope that they did, for the sake of their relationship.

Incidents like this should get a couple talking – or an individual thinking. It's important to know what you want to choose for yourself and what decisions you're willing to leave to someone else. It's also important to consider the issue of reciprocation. If you accept an expensive gift, what (if anything) will you do in return? And what do you think will be expected? If a gift comes with strings attached, it's usually best to decline it. If the giver has a history of dictating the terms, or is manipulative in nature, then you may find yourself in a tricky situation. An ounce of prevention is worth a pound of cure.

Taking on Responsibilities that Aren't Yours

Don't let others make their problems yours – you have enough of your own already. It can be tempting to take on others' responsibilities; feeling needed can give you a nice ego boost. But dependence easily becomes a habit, and soon you'll find yourself resenting people who expect you to solve their problems regularly.

In a post on *The Change Blog*, Ali Hale puts it well when she says that, **"trying to take too much responsibility is a way of putting ourselves at the center of everything."** Please don't misunderstand me. We do favors for friends and family all the time, and vice versa. This is not what I'm referring to (although I do encourage you to put some limits on your favors, so that you still have time for your own priorities). Do those favors, but don't allow others to put you "at the center of everything".

Here's a simple example. A friend has asked to borrow your video camera for her daughter's first recital. You're happy to oblige, assuming she'll call to make an arrangement when she needs it. The day before she needs the camera, she invites you to come over for dinner with it. But you've made other plans; you've been looking forward to this evening for weeks.

When you tell her you're busy tonight, she pleads with you. She explains (in detail) everything that's been going on in her life for the

S

past week, finishing with, "I wouldn't ask you if it hadn't been such a crazy week. I'd be so grateful if you'd help me."

Your friend is disorganized; this is not her first last-minute plea. It hasn't always been convenient, but you haven't given up anything terribly important to help her. If you change your plans and bring the camera to dinner, three things will likely happen:

1. You'll teach her that she can leave things to the last minute and expect you to bail her out, even when you don't want to. The last-minute pleas will continue.
2. You'll resent her for ruining the evening you've been looking forward to for so long.
3. You'll feel angry (and possibly disappointed) with yourself for allowing her to spoil your evening.

This isn't good for you, your friend or your friendship.

Of course, the decision is yours. You may have some reason to accommodate her in spite of the likely consequences; perhaps you feel you owe it to her. If so, be aware that you're helping her to stay dependent. Then decide what your boundaries will be going forward – and communicate them to her. If you're not ready to do that, at least figure out what it will take for you to consider the debt paid. (It's OK if you don't know. You may need to think about it.)

Let's assume you're ready to draw the line. You may have avoided setting a boundary in the past simply because you didn't know how to respond to your friend's pleas. Her desperation and "logic" were too much for you. Fear not. There is a way out.

If it's time to say *no*, then do so firmly and compassionately – and end the conversation. Refuse to engage in any further debate; that's how you end up agreeing to things you don't feel good about. If you've given in before, chances are your friend will continue pleading, giving you all the reasons that he or she can't manage without you.

At this point, you may be tempted to suggest solutions (ask your husband to come past on his way home from work, stop by tomorrow morning, etc.). **Don't do it.**

With people who expect you to exchange your priorities for theirs, proposing solutions usually backfires. They'll give you all kinds of reasons why your solutions won't work, until you're either worn down or convinced that your friend can't solve the problem without you. And without even realizing it, you've taken ownership of someone else's problem. The pattern continues.

The best way to break this cycle is to resist offering too many solutions. Be clear on what you can do to help, and leave it at that. Here are some ideas for dealing with the video camera; feel free to adapt them to fit your own circumstances:

The camera is packed and ready for you. Mark will be up until 10:00; you're welcome to pick it up before then.

I understand that this is important to you; this evening is also important to me. The camera is ready for you. Why don't you think about how to pick it up and call me back? My phone will be on until I leave.

If your friend won't take *no* for an answer, you can say something like this:

I understand. And this is what I can do for you on such short notice.

I know you're feeling desperate right now. And I know that once you calm down, you'll find a way to make it work.

I hear you. And this is what I can do right now. I know that the camera is important to you; my evening is also important to me.

Notice the different approaches you might take when you meet resistance. In the first, you state your boundary and the reason for it (short notice). In the second, you express confidence in your friend's ability to solve the problem. In the third, you reiterate the importance of your plans. However you respond, it's important to end the conversation. Otherwise your friend is likely to wear you down with desperation, guilt trips or other tactics. Consider something like this:

I need to go now. Text me when you've decided what to do.

I trust you'll figure out something. I'm going to get ready now.

I need to get back to work now. Good luck!

Then hang up the phone or walk away. Take a few deep breaths and remind yourself of this important truth:

*It's OK to put your own plans ahead of
someone else's failure to plan.
Really.*

Rescuing Others from Their Own Mistakes

Rescuing is a special case of taking on someone else's responsibilities, but it's worth discussing separately because it's such a common pattern. It can be a tough one to break, especially if you tend to feel sorry for people. It also ensures you have no time for yourself. Allow people to avoid responsibility, and they'll keep avoiding it for years to come. I cannot emphasize this point enough.

Rescuing others from the consequences of their mistakes enables them to keep repeating them. People learn from their mistakes by facing the consequences. This is how we grow. It works that way with our finances, our relationships and just about everything else in life.

Let's take another look at Steve, whose friend Mike has become an alcoholic. Steve feels a deep sense of obligation toward his friend (as well as an unconscious fear of rejection). And that's been enough … until today. Mike has recently extended his binges to Sunday nights. It's now Monday morning, and Mike is too hung over to go to work. He wants Steve to call his boss and lie for him. Just this once. He wouldn't ask if it wasn't so important – and it will never happen again. He's learned his lesson.

What's going on here?

Steve has been rescuing his friend because … well, because he hasn't given too much thought to the situation. Mike calls and he reacts. He sees himself as helping him – but is he? At first, he thought Mike was going through a tough time and that he'd come out of it soon. But it's been months now, and Mike gets himself into trouble every weekend. And now it's affecting his work.

This isn't just a phase, and Mike is not learning from his mistakes.

---

*People learn from their mistakes
by facing the consequences.*

Steve must face the fact that he's not helping his friend at all. Mike needs to face his problem, and Steve isn't doing anything to encourage that. In fact, he's making it easy for Mike to continue. In addiction terms, that's called *enabling*. Steve enables Mike's drinking by making him feel safe. He knows that his buddy will bail him out if things get out of control.

Steve feels he owes Mike. He knows how difficult school would have been without him. He thought it was important to sacrifice for him, that refusing would be disloyal. But now that Mike has asked him to lie, he's taking a long, hard look at the situation.

Yes, good people make sacrifices for others – especially those close to them. But enabling others to continue their destructive patterns is the wrong kind of sacrifice. So is anything that requires you to violate your own values. The purpose of sacrifice is to protect what's important. You give up your Sunday afternoon sports to celebrate Mother's Day. You give up a job you want rather than lie about your qualifications. What you sacrifice must be worth less than what you're protecting. Make sure it isn't the other way around.

Saying Yes to Avoid Feeling Selfish

If you were raised to put others first – or even if it's just what you've always done – taking your own needs into account can be uncomfortable. You may feel selfish, even when you know that what you're doing is right. We humans are naturally afraid of change. Rather than facing our fears and growing, we label what we're afraid of as "bad" and run away from it. That's often why putting ourselves first feels wrong. The mere thought of it triggers fear, and we label it as "selfish" – in other words, "bad". This keeps us in our comfort zones, doing what everyone else wants us to do instead of creating fulfilling lives.

It's important to realize that you don't feel uncomfortable because **you're** wrong. You feel uncomfortable because **something** is wrong. That something may be someone else's excessive demands, or it may be your fear of putting your own needs first. Often people who ask for your help will understand if you decline; it turns out that the pressure is coming from you.

Of course, that's not always the case. Sometimes people let you know subtly that your agreement is expected. They may do this by looking at you in a certain way if you don't go along right away. Or they may use a combination of words, tone of voice and facial expression to express their expectations:

"You'll help me, won't you?" (spoken in a tone of desperation)

"It that a problem?" (accompanied by a disapproving look)

"Do I need to ask someone else?" (in an almost horrified tone with a look to match)

The words, the voice and the expression all let you know that your agreement is expected – and someone's approval is clearly at stake. You may feel selfish, or simply not good enough, if you don't do as expected. If you're not sure what to do, take the time to decide what's right for you. If you're certain that you don't want to go along, ignore the disapproving tone and look. State your decision firmly and stick with it:

"You'll help me, won't you?"

No, I won't be able to help this time.

"It that a problem?"

It is. John and I don't get along, and I'm not willing to spend time with him.

"Do I need to ask someone else?"

Yes, you do. I'm not available on Saturday.

You'll notice that these responses aren't overly polite (and yet not rude, either). Only one of them offers any explanation for your decision. That's because I don't believe in giving too much information to people who use guilt trips to get what they want. They tend to use it against you.

Don't let anyone control you by making you feel bad about yourself. If you're sure that your decision is the right one, then recognize your discomfort for what it is: a sign that **something** is wrong. Don't assume that you're the only problem – or the only solution.

White Liberal Guilt

Please don't take the title literally. You don't need to be white (or even liberal) to experience this type of guilt. Some people feel guilty about being more fortunate than others – especially those who seem to be working hard and getting nowhere. Of course, no one who cares about others can watch this kind of struggle without feeling something. It's just that some of us take it personally, feeling somehow responsible for others' misfortune.

And that's not such a terrible thing, is it? As John F. Kennedy said: "To those whom much is given, much is expected." If no one helps those who struggle to help themselves, the injustice and the suffering will only continue. So how do we find the balance?

It's important to recognize the difference between compassion and guilt. Compassion involves caring for others; guilt involves worrying about ourselves. If you find yourself feeling guilty when you see someone less fortunate that yourself, you need to do something about that. I encourage you to consider therapy and/or quality self-help programs. Unless you are responsible for someone's suffering, guilt is not a healthy response. It shows that, at some level, you don't believe you deserve good things. And since guilt keeps you focused on yourself, your actions are likely to be ineffective.

Now let's look at this from the perspective of boundaries. If helping someone doesn't violate your values or interfere with something you value highly – and you're doing it from compassion rather than misplaced guilt – then it may be worthwhile. If you want to help in a meaningful way, here are some points to consider:

Giving (or even lending) money often enables others to continue their irresponsible behavior. When people have been living beyond their means, a loan won't change that. They need to take responsibility for past mistakes. Taking responsibility isn't only about admitting our mistakes. Anyone can do that. It means taking action: cutting back on expenses, taking a second job or selling unnecessary possessions. In this situation, it's usually better to help someone find ways to increase income or decrease expenses. Remember the statement I made earlier:

People learn from their mistakes
by facing the consequences.

Boundaries are all about respect: for yourself and for others. If others expect you to help them with problems they created themselves, think carefully before going along. Are you respecting yourself and your time? Are you respecting the other as a competent, responsible adult (or young person)? People – especially young people – tend to live up to our expectations of them (when those expectations are reasonable, of course). Don't set the bar too low; you'll deny someone the opportunity to grow.

When you truly respect someone, you're willing to hold her accountable for her actions. You see to it that any help you give respects and encourages her ability to be responsible for herself. That doesn't mean you don't help, or even tolerate bad behavior on occasion. But it does mean that you carefully consider the nature of that help or the extent of that tolerance.

I Should Have ...

"To err is human; to forgive, divine."
from *An Essay on Criticism, Part II*

Alexander Pope, English Poet (1688–1744)

What happens when you realize you've made a mistake? Do you look for the lesson to be learned, or are you too busy beating yourself up over it? Do you apologize, or do you try to shift the blame?

We all know that to err is painfully (and unavoidably) human, yet many of us still strive for perfection. Why is that? What would perfection do for us, if only we could attain it?

According to Brené Brown, we do not admire perfection in others; we prefer authenticity. (Think about it. Don't you feel closer to someone once you see that first crack in the armor?) Yet we're not obsessed with becoming authentic. According to Brown, we chase perfection because we believe it will protect us from shame.

This fear is often unconscious. When you make that report perfect for the boss, you probably don't tell yourself, "I'd better get this right. I don't want to feel ashamed of myself." More likely, you simply tell yourself that it must be good. Maybe you're looking for a promotion or some recognition. Or maybe you're making up for the fact that your last assignment didn't go so well. Whatever the reason, it all comes to down to pain and pleasure. We move toward pleasure (in the form of praise or acknowledgement) and away from pain (feeling ashamed or not good enough).

Being perfect sounds good at first: no mistakes, no shame. But, as I mentioned in the chapter on painful emotions, focusing on what we want to avoid brings us more of the same. Perfectionists judge themselves for every mistake, feeling ashamed when they fail to meet their own unreasonable expectations. They attract the very pain they're trying so hard to avoid.

It's natural to want to avoid pain. What we don't understand is that our pain doesn't come from making mistakes. It comes from expecting ourselves to be something other than human. Dropping that expectation (of ourselves and others) is the fast track to inner peace.

When you let go of the need to be perfect, setting boundaries naturally becomes easier. Putting your needs ahead of others' becomes less painful, as it's no longer necessary to be there for everyone every time. When you accept yourself as you are, guilt trips lose their power. Maybe you are a bit selfish ... once in a while. And maybe that's not so terrible after all.

Putting Guilt in Its Place

Of all the emotions, guilt seems to be the one we struggle with the most. As we've seen in this chapter, we often go to great lengths to escape it. But we aren't meant to escape. Healthy guilt serves a purpose. And when that purpose is fulfilled, we become more than what we were.

Healthy guilt, based on a true understanding of situations and the part we play in them, lets us know that we need to make something right. It tells us that we've violated our own values. It demands action. It pushes us to apologize for being inconsiderate. It forces us to keep our commitments even when it's inconvenient. It encourages us to tell the truth, no matter how difficult that may be. Acting on healthy guilt makes us better people.

When guilt is based on misunderstanding, you can't win. You must choose between "doing the right thing" (even though it really isn't) and honoring your own needs. You take on others' responsibilities and end up resenting them. You do things that don't work for you instead of spending time on the things that matter.

It's important to put guilt in its proper place. Take the time to think about your feelings and understand their source. Question the beliefs attached to your guilt. Ask yourself where your responsibility begins – and where it ends. If there's nothing to feel guilty about, then find the courage to set your boundary and move on. And when the guilt is showing you something you need to change, stop wallowing in all the bad feelings and do something about it. True guilt requires action. With the right action, those awful feelings will fade away. You'll feel better about yourself, because your actions are once again in alignment with your values. That's the purpose of true guilt: to remind you of your highest values and encourage you to live by them.

Even if you're not susceptible to guilt, manipulators still have a few more tricks up their sleeves. In the next chapter, we'll look at four types of pressure that people use to get you to "cave in" – and how to overcome them gracefully.

7TH CHAPTER

WHO'S PRESSURING YOU?

How do you feel when someone tries to push you into something?

"This is the perfect car for us. I know it's expensive, but we need it for the kids. How would you feel if something happened to them because we got something cheaper?"

"I know you're busy, but I really need your help right now. I'm desperate!"

"I won't take *no* for an answer."

"You know how much this means to your mother."

Some people feel angry. Others feel nervous. And others feel so overwhelmed that they give up at the first sign of conflict. How do you react? What gets to you the most?

In this chapter, I'd like to discuss the most common mistakes we make when we're under pressure. All of them are based on faulty assumptions. Once you understand the truth, you'll find it easier to choose a response that works for you.

Giving an Immediate Answer

"Failure to plan on your part does not constitute an emergency on my part." Have you heard this somewhere, or perhaps seen it on a sign in someone's office? It's a popular expression these days. The principle is a good one, even though most of us wouldn't want to respond this way to an actual crisis.

Often people come to us with last-minute requests:

"I need your help right now!"

"We need someone to represent us on the new committee. The first meeting is tomorrow morning. Are you in?"

"The bank won't lend me the money to add on to the house without another signature. Will you sign this for me? I need to close on this today or my builders won't be available until next year."

"Can you stay with the kids for a few extra hours this afternoon? I forgot about a doctor's appointment."

They need an answer **now**. You can feel their anxiety; you have the power to make them feel better instantly. The pressure is on.

Chances are you'd like that pressure to stop. It's uncomfortable. And so is the thought of giving up one of your own priorities. The more intense that conflict becomes, the harder it is to think.

We often say *yes* to make it all go away. But here's the problem: It doesn't. Not really. The other's anxiety certainly stops. The pressure you were feeling stops. But now you're faced with the consequences of your choice. What have you given up to solve someone's last-minute problem? What risk have you taken to satisfy someone else's desires?

If doing this favor is even a little uncomfortable for you, be careful. Saying *yes* isn't just the end of one problem; it's often the beginning of another, potentially larger one. The exchange is seldom a good one.

When something doesn't feel right, insist on taking the time you need to decide. If someone wants your help right now, you can simply say that you're unavailable. If you'd be willing to help later, you can say so. If you need to check your schedule, then do that. If you need to think about cosigning that loan, then good for you! You could end up taking on someone else's debt – or being unable to borrow money for your own needs. Take the time to consider what's at stake and what's important to you. If you decide to take the risk, then you'll be doing so consciously – according to your own values.

When you give in to pressure,
you're more likely to make a bad decision.

Maybe you know that your answer should be *no*, but you can't find the right words. Put it off until you can think more clearly. "I need to think about it," or something to that effect, lets the person know that you might not agree. I recommend giving a timeframe for your decision; anyone who needs to know sooner should look for someone else to help.

Don't let anyone pressure you into deciding too quickly. If you're feeling rushed, you're likely to miss something important. Wait until you're away from the person and have the time to consider things more carefully. At that point, you'll be able to see things in terms of your values. If you're still not sure, you may need more information.

When you have the time you need, you can sort through all of that. When you give in to pressure, you're more likely to make a bad decision. And even if the decision turns out to be a good one, you may not feel good about it – or the person who pressured you.

If you'd like more specific ways to get the time you need, including words you might use, consider reading *7 Easy Ways to Say NO to Almost Anyone.*

Allowing Someone to Wear You Down

I interviewed a woman who was in a manipulative relationship a few years ago. When I asked her how the relationship started, her answer was simple: "He wore me down."

She met this man professionally. When the work was complete, he asked her to take his cell phone number. She didn't want to, but he insisted. She felt uncomfortable refusing a client, even though the work was already done and paid for.

Hours later he called with a dinner invitation. When she refused, he called again. And again. His calls were sometimes only ten minutes apart. She found this irritating and ignored his calls. But they kept coming. After a while she answered, just to tell him to stop calling. This had no effect. She finally agreed to dinner to shut him up.

Looking back, she realized that she had all the power. She could have refused to answer any further calls. He didn't have her address; her cell phone was his only way to reach her. She gave away her power without even realizing she had it.

There's nothing charming about this level of persistence. People who repeatedly harass you with the same request, ignoring your clearly stated boundary, are not respecting you. This is the behavior of children; it is **not** a good sign in adults.

If someone is trying to wear you down, be firm. Hang up the phone or walk away. Refuse to discuss it further: *You have my answer. I'm not changing my mind, and I'm not talking about it again.* If necessary, avoid (or at least minimize) contact with the person until he or she is prepared to respect your boundary (or it becomes irrelevant). Of course, this won't always be possible – or the right thing to do. But it's worth considering when all else fails.

Sometimes the person wearing you down is a friend or relative. Linda's friend Vicki insists that they go out for dinner on Saturday. Linda has made it clear that she's too busy. She has even talked about her projects and deadlines so that her friend won't feel ignored. But that just made her more determined:

"You need to relax. An evening out is just what the doctor ordered."

I can't relax right now. I have too many deadlines.

"We'll talk about movies we've seen and where we want to go on vacation this year. I promise ... nothing heavy."

But Linda knows better; Vicki will break that promise in the first five minutes. ("I need your advice on something quickly....") And an evening of listening to Vicki's problems is anything but relaxing. She's been there too many times.

But how can Linda tell Vicki that an evening with her won't be relaxing?

She doesn't have to. Her decision is her own, and there's no need to justify it any further. When her friend insists, she can simply reiterate that she doesn't have the time right now – and reinforce that by saying goodbye.

I appreciate that, Vicki. But I'm not going out this weekend. I've gotta go now. I'll give you a call next week when things are quieter.

At least until her deadlines are past, Linda can make conscious decisions about answering or returning Vicki's phone calls.

Karen's situation is a bit different. Her weekends are free – freer than she would like, in fact. Her brother and sister-in-law have invited her to join them on their boat, but she hates being on the water. Her brother's requests have become more insistent, and she's running out of excuses. How does she get out of this diplomatically?

The answer is simple. It's time for Karen to stop making excuses and tell the truth: *Ron, I would really love to see you and Brenda. I'm just not willing to go out on the water again. I should have told you sooner, but I thought it would be rude, or that you might try to convince me to change my mind. I would be happy to join you for drinks or dinner when you're done on the boat.*

Now Ron understands Karen's boundary. He no longer needs to wonder whether she's avoiding him. And suggesting an alternative allows her to follow the *no* with a *yes*. Everyone wins.

Someone who won't take *no* for an answer is sending you a message: "I won't stop until you give me what I want." In the case of

Linda's friend, dinner can wait. When it comes to Karen and her brother, a little honesty goes a long way.

Don't let others make your decisions; do what's right for you. There may be times when others refuse to accept your choices. That's OK. Their approval would be nice, but you'll manage without it.

Believing It Must Be Important

When people pressure us, it can be easy to think that the issue must be important. Why else would they invest so much energy – and make things so unpleasant for us? If the person pressuring you is an important part of your life and doesn't often act this way, you may be right. Ask what makes this so important. Why is he or she so insistent on changing your mind?

People may pressure you for many reasons.
But these reasons have nothing to do with
you or your values.

But in any other situation, I encourage you to let go of this idea. People will pressure you for many reasons. They may want what they want, no matter how it affects you. They may "know" that they're right, regardless of what you think. They could simply be more willing to push you into something you don't want than they are to do the work themselves. They may see you as the only way to reach their goal, simply because they haven't taken the time to explore other options. None of these reasons has anything to do with you or your values.

Consider Patricia, who is balancing family obligations with studying law part-time. A member of her study group has asked her to do part of his work, with the promise that he'll make it up to her as soon as he's done with another assignment. Let's listen in on their conversation:

"I'm really struggling with a project that's due in less than a week; it's a lot harder than I expected. If you'll do my work for the study group this week, I'll do something of yours as soon as I'm finished. I'll do even more than what you're doing for me, I promise."

You might think I'm not as busy as you are because I'm only part-time, but I have a family to look after. I'll look at my schedule and get back to you.

"Please, Patricia. I know you're busy, too, but I really need your help – and I'll more than make it up to you."

I told you I'll have to think about it. If you need an answer right now, then ask someone else.

"You know I can't! Everyone else is busy with the same project."

Then you'll have to wait for me to get back to you.

Patricia walks away, giving herself time to consider what she might be willing to do for her classmate and what she wants in return.

The fact that someone gets intense with you doesn't mean that what he wants is aligned with your values. Remember to consider what's important to you before giving your answer.

Trying to Make Everyone Happy

Sometimes there's no one harassing you, no one who will express outright disapproval if you don't go along. The pressure comes from within. It's important to find the source of that pressure and heal the pain and false beliefs behind it.

One of those beliefs is that we need to keep everyone happy. You may have learned this simply by watching a parent accommodate everyone, regardless of the personal cost. Or you may have painful memories of the price of failure. (Were you and your siblings beaten or humiliated when a parent was angry with you? Was one of them an alcoholic, prone to dangerous rages?) Or you may believe that keeping everyone happy is the only way you'll be accepted. Whatever the reason, it's important to deal with it.

Trying to keep everyone happy is a disservice to them as well as to yourself. Our need to do this is based on some major misconceptions:

1. *It's possible to keep everyone happy.* This is simply not true. Even if you give up your own needs (which means that not everyone is happy), you still can't guarantee that everyone else will be happy. Eventually their demands on you will conflict. What then?

2. *Keeping everyone happy makes you a good person.* Looking after everyone else's immediate desires, rescuing them from their own mistakes and keeping them dependent on you does not make you a good person. Being "good" isn't that easy. Sometimes we need to allow others to learn from their mistakes. And handling disappointment is an important part of life. We all need to learn that we can't always get what we want. Placing your need for approval above all of that doesn't qualify you for a medal.

3. *Keeping others happy will make you feel good.* Another lie! Keeping others happy will put an end to any unpleasant feelings that arise when you consider putting your own needs first. But the relief will be short-lived. That's because keeping everyone else happy usually means ignoring your own needs. This sends a message to your unconscious that you're not important – and possibly that you're willing to violate your highest values. Neither of these feels good, and neither will go away until you make the necessary changes.

Wait, there's more! Depending on the approval of others for your good feelings is a bad strategy. In a good relationship, you are loved and accepted as you are (although there may be moments when it doesn't seem that way). You don't need to earn that acceptance through regular sacrifices. In a manipulative relationship, approval lasts as long as your compliance. As soon as you do what's best for you (or choose one person's demands over another's), someone's approval disappears – and so do those good feelings.

There is only one reliable way to feel good about yourself: Act according to your own highest values, and do so consistently. Only when your choices are in line your values will you truly see yourself as a good person.

Once you accept that it's not possible (or even good) to keep everyone happy all the time, you can start living your life according to what's best for you. Follow your values and you won't go wrong.

Deal with It

When people pressure us, we can feel very uncomfortable. Our first impulse is to make that discomfort go away. But because our perspective is so limited (we want to make it go away now, regardless of the consequences), the discomfort always returns. The solution is to deal with the true causes of that discomfort so that it (and the people connected to it) can no longer control you.

Fortunately, others don't cause that discomfort; they merely trigger it. The real pressure comes from within. Unless it's a real emergency (the kind you couldn't see coming), someone who needs an immediate answer has waited too long. Don't take on their panic – or their expectation that you'll come to the rescue. It's OK if you can't decide right now.

The same is true for people who wear you down. It is the combination of your emotions and beliefs that gives them their power. If you're comfortable saying *no*, there's no problem. Don't allow the conversation to continue and they won't be able to wear you down. Accept that you can't make everyone happy and move on.

Of course, some tactics are a bit more subtle than outright pressure. And sometimes, without even realizing it, we make it easy for people to take advantage. In the next chapter, we'll look at three ways you may be giving people permission to ignore your boundaries.

8ᵀᴴ CHAPTER

DO YOU GIVE IN TOO SOON?

In the wealth-building classic *Think and Grow Rich,* Napoleon Hill tells the story of a man who almost made millions during the gold rush. He and his uncle borrowed money from family and friends and staked a claim. They started digging, and it looked like they'd found one of the best mines in Colorado. Soon they'd be rich!

And then the unthinkable happened: the gold ran out. The vein disappeared. They dug and dug, but to no avail. After many attempts, they gave up. They sold their equipment to a junk man and went home.

The junk man, being a bit smarter than these two men, hired a mining engineer. After some calculations, the engineer told him that the vein was three feet from where the two had been digging. He made millions from that mine.

Giving in to Resistance

Success seldom comes to those who quietly wish for it – or even those who ask for it. It comes to those who persist. Giving in too easily is one of the most common mistakes we make.

Patricia, whom we met in the last chapter, had to learn to stand her ground with her teenagers before she could start law school.

Two years ago, she decided she wanted to start work as a paralegal as soon as the last of her children left for college. She applied to a nearby university. It would take her four years to complete her associate's degree part-time, so she wanted to start soon.

She spoke to her husband about it, and he agreed. The school she wanted was expensive, but they could afford it. Her two children were also supportive – until she explained what it would mean to them:

- They might need to make dinner or clean up during exams and big projects.
- There would be fewer weekend pool parties, as Mom might not be available to supervise.
- Family vacations would be within driving distance. No more skiing in Aspen or swimming in the Caribbean until Mom finished her degree.

The looks on their faces said it all. Patricia began to doubt her dream. How could she expect her children to sacrifice for her? Wasn't that her role as a mother? She looked to her husband for support, but he was quiet.

Resistance comes in many forms. Patricia wasn't prepared for the shock on her children's faces. And she wasn't sure how to interpret her husband's silence. After much contemplation, she decided that her dream was too important to lose. She met with her family again. This time she talked about how much she had sacrificed to be a full-time mom, and how important this career was to her. She gave everyone the chance to share their feelings. In the end, they all agreed that she should begin her studies as soon as possible.

The key to handling resistance is to remember the purpose of your boundary and what it's worth to you. When something important is at stake, focusing on that will help you to find the courage to stand by your decision.

Giving Up When Your Boundary Is Ignored

Everything went smoothly for a while. Patricia did well on her midterm exams, and her family gave her the time she needed for her studies. But then one of her classes became more difficult; she struggled with the material. She joined a study group that met two evenings a week, and for the first time the family had to deal with dinner without her.

It was up to her daughter to make a simple meal. Her son's task was to set the table and clean up afterwards. When she came home, she found the dirty dishes all over the kitchen counter. Her son seemed to think that setting the table and clearing it was enough. Her daughter had been instructed to make spaghetti and meatballs for dinner; there was no sign of the meatballs.

Patricia's children supported her decision – until it meant extra work for them. This pattern isn't limited to children. Many adults will behave in the same way, supporting you right up until the moment your decision is inconvenient for them. This is where so many people fail. They state their boundary, convince others to support it and assume that they're done. But setting the boundary is only the beginning.

Personal boundaries are no different than physical ones.

Imagine that you put an expensive fence around your vegetable garden to keep the rabbits out. One day you come home from work to discover a nice big hole in the fence – and no more lettuce. Would you give up on growing vegetables, or would you repair the fence? If you planted the garden under duress, believing it was a waste of time, you might be inclined to give up. You might even feel vindicated: "I told you this was a bad idea!" But if that garden is important to you, you'll repair the fence. And you'll figure out how to keep those rabbits from gnawing through it again. You'll invest time and effort in protecting that garden because it's important to you.

Personal boundaries are no different than physical ones. When your goal matters more to you than the discomfort involved in protecting it, you'll do what needs to be done. Manipulators can only get their way by making that discomfort more important than your boundary.

Patricia and her husband discussed the situation. They decided to give their children a lesson in responsibility. Both of them were grounded. And twice a week Patricia left them written instructions – with a reminder that they would lose their allowances if they didn't fulfill their responsibilities on either of the days. Suddenly there were meatballs with the spaghetti and everything was cleaned up nicely when Patricia came home.

If something matters to you, don't give up at the first sign of resistance. Stay focused on what's important and find a way to protect your boundary.

Not Making Your Boundary Real

As I mentioned in the introduction, a boundary isn't a boundary without consequences.

"You can't speak to me that way," draws a line in the sand. But when the line is crossed and nothing happens, it turns out that what looked like a boundary was only a preference. The message is clear: "I wish you wouldn't speak to me that way, but I don't have the courage to stop you. You can do as you please."

This is the message Kyra sent to her friends when they continued calling her in the morning. Although she would let them know she was busy, in the end she would sigh and give in. She had naïvely expected them to simply respect her wishes. If she had made her boundary real by refusing to answer her phone until she was ready, she wouldn't have had a problem.

When a child disobeys his parents, he gets a warning: "Don't do that again!" When he continues to engage in the forbidden behavior, there must be consequences. Otherwise he'll learn that the rules don't apply to him.

Adults learn in the same way. When you're dealing with someone whose interests conflict with yours, consequences may be the only thing stopping her from trampling all over you and your boundary. They may be used in two ways:

- to make sure it can't happen again, or
- to convince others to change their behavior.

For example, Lisa's husband likes to make jokes at her expense. She doesn't mind so much when they're alone, but she hates it when he does it in front of people. She has told him so several times, but he tells her she's being too sensitive. She has asked him to respect her feelings anyway, but he refuses. Making sure it can't happen again would mean refusing to attend his family's get-togethers until he stops. It would also mean going to her own without him – or missing them altogether. Her only alternative is to convince him not to do it again. Since asking repeatedly has failed, she'll need to make use of consequences.

Lisa knows that her husband takes his image as the "good guy" seriously. So, at the next family get-together, she responds to her husband's first joke by calling him on it: *Tom, I've told you how uncomfortable I feel when you put me down like that – even as a joke. Please stop.*

Tom turns red and walks away. Yes, he's angry and embarrassed, but he gets the message: Lisa has had enough. He can no longer afford to ignore her feelings.

Consequences aren't always about words, and they're not always explicit. If you've told someone repeatedly that you need a full day's notice, then stop rearranging your schedule for his last-minute requests. (If he's a client, consider charging a premium for them.) If your teenager consistently forgets to tell you about things that require your time (for example, driving her somewhere), then refuse once. Remind her that she needed to tell you the night before. She'll miss out on something she was looking forward to, and she won't let that happen again. We teach people how to treat us, whether they're 15 or 50.

What You Resist Persists

We often give up on what's important to us because we don't want to deal with something. Whether we're afraid of confrontation, guilt or something else, we'd rather sacrifice what we care about than face our feelings. But running away isn't the answer. Until we face our fears, our lives are not our own. Your priorities are worth protecting. Don't give up when the gold is only three feet away.

We've explored a lot of ways that we hand our power to others – and many of our reasons for doing it. But before we close, I'd like to talk about something completely different. In the next chapter, you'll learn how to tell when you don't need a boundary after all – even though it may feel like you do.

9TH CHAPTER

DO YOU NEED A BOUNDARY?

"Asserting yourself when all that is required is kindness and compassion isn't assertiveness at all...." – Tiny Buddha

By this point, you've invested a lot of time and energy learning to set healthy boundaries. As I've mentioned earlier, boundaries protect what's important to you. And good, respectful boundaries will only improve most relationships. But this book would not be complete if I failed to mention that setting a boundary isn't always the best approach, even when it's tempting. Here are some situations to consider:

- The relationship is more important than the issue.
- Compromise is a better option.
- Your power is limited.
- The risk is too great.
- You don't want to continue the relationship.
- Silence is more effective.

Let's look at some examples of each.

The Relationship is More Important than the Issue

Linda is at her cousin's wedding reception, chatting with her aunt Rose about the groom, when her mother joins them. Rose shares a story about Quinton helping a stranger find his way to a job interview, saying that Sara knew then that this was the man she'd been waiting for.

"Well," quips Linda's mother, "maybe we should ask Quinton and Sara to give my son a place to stay. Kindness is such a rare quality these days." She gives Rose a knowing look.

Setting a boundary isn't always the best approach,
even when it's tempting.

Linda feels her face flush. Did Rose – and everyone else in the family, for that matter – really think she was selfish for not wanting her brother to stay with her? Or was her mother just trying to make her think so? She's torn between telling her mother off (including some choice words about the lazy mama's boy she raised) and running away.

Before Linda's thoughts can race any further, Rose smiles cheerfully. "Finally," she says, "the perfect solution! I'll go tell the bride the good news!"

Linda takes a deep breath and smiles at her aunt's humor. Rose always knew the right thing to say. "Speaking of living arrangements, Aunt Rose, where did you say they were looking to buy? I hope it's not too far from you." The three of them talk about neighborhoods, the outrageous price of properties and the challenge of finding the right area to raise a family. Everyone is happy again, and the subject of Linda's unemployed brother is forgotten.

On her way home from the reception, Linda still wants to give her mother a piece of her mind. She considers confronting her privately about the guilt trips, but she knows she wouldn't be open to the conversation. And it's not necessary. The end of the month is less than a week away, and Linda must make up her mind in the next few days.

This is a tough time for both of them. Talking about it can wait until she has made her decision. She's considering allowing her brother to stay for a single month, after which he would have to find somewhere else. She needs another day or two to think it over.

It's important to understand what your boundary will protect. When it's nothing more than your ego, think carefully before you speak. Is it worth damaging a relationship? Some situations deserve a bit more patience than others. Before you set a boundary with someone important to you, be sure it's the right one – and consider whether a little more compassion isn't the best response.

Compromise Is a Better Option

Setting boundaries is a good way to protect what's important to you. But what about others? Sometimes we need to balance what's important to us with what's important to the people we care about. It's easy to get stuck in the belief that we must choose one or the other, but often there's a way to meet everyone's needs. We just need to look for it.

Lisa is still feeling angry and hurt about her sister's choice of restaurant; she's considering boycotting the event to make her point. But her best friend has convinced her to talk to her sister directly – and to do so as nicely as possible. Lisa doesn't expect it to help, but she agrees to try.

When she finally makes the call, she learns that the restaurant is under new management, with a much larger menu. Her sister thought she knew, as she'd discussed this with their mother. No longer feeling slighted, Lisa agrees to give the new menu a try. She makes a mental note to speak to her sister directly the next time she's upset with her. Her sister resolves to make sure that Lisa is included in all family decisions, even when it seems unnecessary.

Patricia is studying for exams, and her mother wants to celebrate her father's 65th birthday this weekend – at Patricia's home. In the past, Patricia has hosted all the family get-togethers. As a stay-at-home mom and the wealthiest member of the family, she would organize everything. Then her sisters and her mother would help in the kitchen and everyone would pitch in with the cleanup. But now she has neither the time nor the money to throw a big party.

Her first reaction is anger and hurt. Doesn't her mother take her degree seriously? Does she think she can just press the pause button on her studies for the rest of the week? Not wanting to say something she'd regret, she tells her mother she'll call her back in a little while.

When she feels calmer, Patricia becomes aware of several options. Someone else could host the party, although she wasn't sure who that would be. They could go to a restaurant – if her brothers and sisters paid their fair share. She could spend a few hours there and then leave on her own to study. Or they could postpone the celebration until her exams were over – and her nephew would be home from school as well. She could host it then, if her brothers and sisters were willing to share the cost.

Patricia calls her mother, and they agree that her father would want his grandson to be there – and his daughter to enjoy herself without worrying about exams. They choose a date, and she calls the rest of the family to discuss the arrangements. No one minds contributing financially, and one of her sisters even offers to help her pick up the food and party supplies in the morning.

Sometimes – especially when we feel hurt or angry – we forget that compromise is not inconsistent with healthy boundaries. To find a good compromise, you must know the difference between necessities and preferences. Patricia didn't want to attend a party on the weekend, but she was willing to do it for her father. She didn't have the time to host the party herself before exams; so that part wasn't negotiable. Once her mother understood the situation, and what Patricia was willing to do, they could come up with something that worked for everyone.

Your Power Is Limited

Sometimes we're not able to set a boundary. Consider Diane, who wants to hear her favorite author speak tonight. Her husband is away on business, and it's too late to hire a babysitter. Her only option is to ask her mother. But she knows that Granny will arrive with a purse full of sweets and let the children watch too much TV.

In the past, Diane would have laid down the law and expected her mother to honor her wishes. But after one fight too many, she realized that she couldn't control her mother. So even though money is tight, she hires a babysitter when she needs one. The kids go to bed on time, and they don't get any extra sugar.

But it's too late for a babysitter, and she wants a signed copy of that author's latest book. So she bakes a batch of the kids' favorite cookies – her own healthy, low-sugar recipe. She leaves them out, hoping the kids will eat them instead of Granny's sweets. And she leaves early to get a seat near the front. Once that book is signed, she's going straight home.

Diane has learned to manage both her mother and her children without unnecessary conflict. She knows that none of them will honor her wishes when it comes to sugar or TV. But she can minimize the damage. Rather than trying to change her mother, who sees no reason to change, she accepts her as she is and acts accordingly. She hires babysitters when she can, and bakes healthy treats when she can't. As for the TV, it's just one night and she'll get home as early as she can.

Sometimes a boundary is impossible to enforce. When you can't control a situation, either avoid it or do what you can to influence it – and let go of the rest. You'll be happier for it.

The Risk Is Too Great

Sometimes a situation seems to scream for a boundary – and the sooner the better. We're tempted to set that boundary in a moment of anger or stubbornness, putting our physical or emotional well-being at risk.

Lisa's boss has suddenly become aggressive and demanding. He expects her to stay late every evening doing work that isn't in her job description; he calls every weekend with office emergencies, few of which are hers. When she refuses, which she only does when she has family obligations, he becomes abusive. She has tried to reason with him, but he won't listen. He wants the job done, and he doesn't want to hear any excuses.

*Setting a boundary doesn't work
with unreasonable people.*

Lisa has almost told him off several times, but she can't afford to lose her job. The mortgage payments are greater than her husband's take-home pay, and they have no savings to speak of. Lisa is not at all confident that she would succeed with a formal complaint. She has seen her boss lie (quite convincingly), and there is no one to back up her story. It's important that she not lose her temper and do something she regrets.

Setting a boundary doesn't work with unreasonable people. In such situations, the two major options are to leave or to appeal to others who are more reasonable. Given the likelihood that her boss will lie and get away with it, Lisa would be wise to look for another job. She could also consider speaking to a labor lawyer. She needs to know her rights as well as her chances of winning a dispute with her company. What proof would she need, and how would she get it? If she gets that proof, she may decide to file a complaint. In the meantime, she may need to find some short-term ways to cope with her boss' demands. Her situation is unlikely to be resolved overnight.

If Lisa cannot prove her case, walking away may be her best option. This can be a hard choice, as it feels like losing. But what's more important: a short-term workplace battle or her long-term happiness?

You Don't Want to Continue the Relationship

If you dislike someone and don't want to spend any more time together, why bother setting boundaries? Boundaries are about what you'll accept and what you won't in an interaction or relationship. If you'd be willing to continue if a few things changed, explore that. But otherwise, what's the point?

Let's look at an example to better understand this principle. Marie has spoken to a divorce lawyer, so she knows what to expect if she leaves Hal. Although she's still worried about her mother's reaction, she is seriously considering leaving. It would be tough, but she knows that she can manage.

But Marie was once in love with Hal, and she believes that he was in love with her. She would like to renew their relationship. Marie must decide where her boundary lies. What does she want from their relationship? What's essential and what's nice to have? How will she know when she has it? And how patient is she willing to be? Has she reached the point where counselling is the only way, or is she willing to work with Hal without any outside help? Once she has answered these questions, she'll be able to share her feelings – and her boundaries – with Hal. It's worth the trouble because she wants to make things work. And she won't know until she tries.

Marie starts a part-time job, despite Hal's objections. Hal eventually agrees to counselling, but stops going after a few months. "You're trying to solve a problem that doesn't exist," he complains. "Everything's fine."

Marie continues with therapy, as she needs the emotional support. Hal gives lip service to their relationship, but he's not interested.

After a few more months, Marie concludes that he wants to keep the family together, but he's not interested in having a meaningful relationship with her.

The time for setting boundaries has past. Now it's time for action. If Marie is ever going to be happy, she needs to insist on a divorce.

Of course, not all relationships are this important. Sometimes staying away is easy, as is the case with casual acquaintances or negative people at the office (unless you work with them, of course). Before you start choosing your boundaries, remember to ask yourself this important question: Do I want (or need) to be in this relationship? If not, consider forgetting about the rest of the boundaries and putting some distance between yourself and the other person.

Silence Is Just as Effective

Do you remember Diane's mother, the one who makes cookies for the grandchildren and lets them watch TV all night? What you may have forgotten is that she's also the one who tries to sabotage date night. Here's her latest burst of resentment, shared at a family get-together:

"Let's get together for dinner next Friday. The weekends are always so busy for everyone."

Mom, you know I can't make it on a Friday night.

"Oh, that's right. How could I forget? Diane is more special than the rest of us; she has a day of the week reserved just for her. We mustn't interfere with that, no matter how inconvenient it might be for the rest of us."

All eyes are on Diane, waiting for her response. She turns to her sister and asks if dinner on Saturday or lunch on Sunday would work for her. She then asks everyone else, ending with her mother.

When her mother got in yet another dig about date night, Diane's first impulse was to set her straight. She wanted to tell her to cut the sarcasm and act like an adult. Why couldn't she just be happy for her?

Then, out of the corner of her eye, she saw her father and uncle watching the game. She remembered how strained her parents' relationship was, how hard her mother tried to get this man's attention. She took a deep breath and ignored her mother's sarcasm. This was neither the time nor the place to deal with it. She would wait until she felt calmer and decide how to move forward. For now, she would let it go.

Sometimes silence is the best response. We don't need to defend ourselves against every rude remark – even those designed to hurt us. We can breathe and move on, secure in our own truth.

Another time we may choose to stay quiet is when others are saying things we don't agree with. For example, if someone makes an ugly remark, silence may convey your disapproval far more effectively than words. The same is true for many of the things we find offensive. If you are the leader of a group and a member insults another member, you'll need to make it clear that you won't tolerate that. But if you're with family or colleagues, or meeting new people at a party, you may decide to keep quiet – or walk away.

Many years ago, I was involved in a conversation with someone who tried to convince me that I should get a gun and learn how to use it, because the day was coming when I would need it. He would be able to protect his family and his belongings – what about me? We argued about this for quite a while, and I did not enjoy the conversation. Later that day I was with a friend of a friend who seemed to share my views, and I asked him how to respond to that man. How could I convince him that violence wasn't the answer?

I never forgot his simple, straightforward response: "Why do you need to?"

I could have avoided all that unpleasantness by refusing to argue. Instead of making my points and feeling frustrated, I could have changed the subject. If he continued, silence or short acknowledgements like, "I hear you," could have brought the conversation to an end. We didn't need to agree. I didn't need to –

nor could I – convince him of anything. Understanding that makes life a lot easier.

Sometimes the best thing to say is nothing at all. Consider this the next time you're choosing your response in a difficult situation.

Think Before You Set Your Boundary

Certain boundaries are important. We all deserve to decide how to spend our time and money, what limits to place on our children, and how much we'll sacrifice for others. But when the consequences may be unpleasant, or it's important to consider others' needs, it pays to think carefully before acting. The purpose of a boundary is to protect what's important to you. Make sure it will do just that.

10TH CHAPTER

IT DOESN'T HAPPEN BY ITSELF

As you can see, healthy boundaries don't happen by themselves. There are many obstacles to be overcome, many old patterns to break. Considering them all can be overwhelming! Fortunately, there's no need to do that. Just find the area that most needs your attention and start there. Don't worry about the rest until you've made some progress. To make it easier for you to get started, here's a summary of the types of obstacles you may be facing:

Knowing and Trusting Yourself

Knowing yourself means understanding what's important to you in various situations. We set boundaries to protect what matters most to us. If you don't know what that is, how can you be happy? If this is where your problem lies, focus here first. There's no point in learning how to better communicate a boundary if you don't know what it should be in the first place.

When you trust yourself, you're able to live according to your own values rather than someone else's. This is the key to happiness. When we betray those values, we don't feel good about ourselves. And no amount of excuses or self-deception will change that.

Sometimes honoring our values means accepting a truth that we'd rather not face. That truth may be unpleasant: *My new friend expects me to drop everything for her, but she won't do the same for me. It's time to move on.*

Or it may be much more difficult: *My husband is cheating on me again. He's not going to change, no matter how often he apologizes or how much he wants me to stay.*

Sometimes it means dealing with our inner conflicts: *I like feeling needed, but I want some time for myself.* Knowing yourself is an ongoing process. Exploring your need to be needed – or any other reason you may have for doing things that don't work for you – will help you to know yourself better and make better choices.

Knowing and trusting yourself is the foundation for setting good boundaries. If you feel you need to strengthen that foundation, then this is the place to start.

Your Beliefs and Expectations

False beliefs and unrealistic expectations are one of the biggest reasons for unhappiness in relationships. Here we've focused on the ones that stop us from setting healthy boundaries.

One of the most basic assumptions we make in close relationships is that others share and respect our values. The people closest to us **know** where we draw the line – and they would never overstep it. This isn't always the case. If a boundary is important to you, don't assume that everyone understands and supports it.

Another common obstacle is the belief that we should put others' needs before our own. Yes, altruism is good for the soul – when it supports your highest values. Sacrificing for your children and looking after an aging parent are good examples of this. But we often put others first because we believe that they matter more, they can't do without us or we can't handle the consequences of setting a healthy boundary. That's not altruism at all; it's just plain fear. If you're going to feel good about yourself and your life, you need to move past that fear. You don't need to do it all at once; it's OK to take baby steps.

It's also easy to minimize or make excuses for others' behavior: *He must have a good reason for lying to me. It won't be like this forever. It will all be worth it later. It's just one little thing* (but is it really?). And it's just as easy to give up: *I can't do anything about it, so why bother? I'd rather keep the peace.*

Some of us even have beliefs about the word *no*. We may see it as harsh or hurtful. And how many of us have that one person we can't refuse?

Getting through these obstacles is all about letting go of the lies. Others **can** do without you; they simply prefer not to. You matter as much as they do, and not one bit less. And of course he had a good reason for lying to you – but the fact that it was good enough for him doesn't mean it's good enough for you!

If you're still believing some of these lies, then get to work. Whenever you're ready to agree to something that doesn't suit you, question yourself. What's behind your decision? What belief or value is driving it? And, most importantly, is it real? Is this the truth?

How You Communicate

Sometimes we know what's important and what boundary to set, but we don't communicate it effectively. This can be harder to spot, as we all tend to assume that we made ourselves perfectly clear. But with a little patience, you can still figure out what's happening.

Sometimes we diminish our message by the way in which we deliver it. There are many ways to do this:

- being too polite;
- being afraid to repeat yourself;
- speaking hesitantly;
- smiling, laughing or looking away as you speak; or
- filling the silence with excuses for your boundary.

These behaviors can send the message that you're unsure of yourself and therefore won't defend your boundary. Letting someone else control the conversation has a similar effect, as your boundary gets buried in the other person's blaming, excuses or empty promises. Once your message has lost its power, many people feel comfortable ignoring your wants and needs. If you're being understood but not getting what you want, this may be the reason. Of course, it may be that the people you're dealing with simply aren't interested in accommodating you, regardless of how well you express yourself.

If your boundary is important, deliver it with confidence – or at least your best attempt. Don't let anyone distract you from your message or stop you from taking action when your boundary is ignored.

Sometimes others don't understand your boundary. If people who have no ulterior motives claim not to understand, then chances are they don't. When you're dealing with people who care about you, it may help to explain what your boundary protects (family time, privacy, etc.). This will clarify any confusion – and help them to understand what makes this so important to you.

Of course, manipulative people often pretend not to understand; that way they can shift the blame to you. Start noticing when that misunderstanding is all too convenient.

If you suspect you're not communicating in the best way possible, pay attention to what you say, how you say it, and how others respond. In time, some patterns will emerge and you'll see what you need to do differently.

Avoiding Pain

We often avoid setting the boundaries we really need because we find it too painful. Some of us are afraid of confrontation. (Being subjected to emotional or physical abuse has that effect.) Others will agree to almost anything to avoid experiencing shame, rejection or some other form of emotional pain. Some people imagine the worst possible consequences to standing up for themselves and give in to those unfounded fears. Others get so sucked into the dramas around them that they simply have to make things better. These people are running from their emotions; anyone who can make them feel badly enough can control them.

At some level, we're all afraid of pain and suffering. If you've allowed this to dictate your decisions, then it's time to face your fears and take your power back.

Chasing Agreement and Approval

We all want to be noticed. We all want others to agree with us and, even more importantly, to approve of us. We want others to see us as inherently good (or even special). The question is: How far are we willing to go to convince them to give us what we want?

When we're seeking approval, we're vulnerable to manipulation – but remember that it's a two-way street. What will you do to please that person? What will you say to make him think you're clever? How far will you go for that approving look – the one that says you're the best (at least for the moment)?

If you want approval but are prepared to manage without it, you can still make choices that work for you. The trouble begins when that desire feels like a need. So how do you know whether your desire for approval makes you vulnerable? How much is too much?

Although knowing yourself is much more art than science, there are some clues that you might be making other people's opinions too important:

1. When people are sharing their opinions on something, you wait until you have a sense of what the group believes. If your opinion seems different, you keep quiet.

2. You often find yourself agreeing to things you don't want to do, whether they're favors or things you don't enjoy. It just seems easier to go along.

3. You tend to play conversations out in your mind ahead of time. You think about how people will react and do your best to appear smart, well-informed or kind-hearted – however you'd like to be seen by others.

4. During conversations, you often find yourself wondering about others' reactions:

    *   *He looks so serious. Did I say something wrong?*

    *   *She hasn't smiled at me once. Is she angry with me?*

    *   *He's laughing. Does that mean he likes my jokes – or does he think I'm an idiot?*

5. You review social conversations in your mind, focusing on how people reacted to you.

6. If someone doesn't seem to like what you've said, you're ready with an explanation or qualification. *I went for a massage yesterday … because my back was sore.*

7. You carefully adjust what you share to fit the mood of the listener(s) – and pretend to be interested in topics that really don't work for you.

8. While others are talking, part of you is busy trying to figure out what to say next. And, although this isn't always conscious, your next remark is intended to prove something about you: your intelligence, your interest in the other, or anything else you'd like them to see.

If you find yourself engaging in any of these behaviors regularly, you're probably more concerned about what others think of you than what you think of yourself. If that's the case, then this might be a good place for you to put your attention.

Guilt, Obligation and Responsibility

Guilt is one of the most painful emotions there is … which makes it one of our most powerful motivators. How many of us can honestly say we've never done something we didn't want to do because we felt obligated? Accepting gifts or favors can intensify this sense of obligation. And regardless of the original cause, guilt can lead us to take on responsibilities that were never ours – including rescuing others from their own mistakes rather than allowing them to learn from the experience. And sometimes our unrealistic expectations of ourselves (nothing less than perfection will do!) leave us feeling so inadequate that we'll do almost anything to avoid feeling worse. We'll say *yes* to just about anything to avoid being seen as selfish or uncaring.

To deal with these issues, you need an understanding of human dynamics – along with some good old-fashioned self-esteem. If guilt trips work all too well on you, then figure out what's going on inside yourself. Are you falling for faulty logic, or is low self-esteem the problem?

If it's the logic, review the chapter on guilt and apply each principle to your own life. Focus on the ones that seem most relevant to you. If you understand the principles but don't have the confidence to apply them, then work on that.

We all have the right to feel good about ourselves and our choices – especially the choices that support our highest values. If you feel guilty doing what you know is right, or feel selfish putting your own needs before anyone else's, then do something about it. Get whatever help you need; you're worth the trouble.

Giving in to Pressure

For some of us, setting boundaries isn't that hard most of the time. But with certain people, or in certain situations, the pressure is too much. They need an answer right now – and they won't leave us alone until we give in.

If you find yourself giving in to pressure, consider your reasons. Here are some questions to ask yourself:

- Is confrontation too painful for you? (If so, go back to the chapter on emotional pain.)
- Do you think that it must be important, or the other wouldn't be pressuring you like this? (If so, go back to the chapter on unrealistic beliefs and expectations and consider whether this is true.)
- Are your excuses for saying *no* being turned against you? (If so, you may be too dependent on others for approval.)

Giving in to pressure is all about putting other people's desires ahead of our own values. When we don't make our own values a priority, there's always a reason. Find it and deal with it. Until you do, you won't be able to live the life that's meant for you.

Giving Up Too Soon

One of the toughest things about boundaries is that they don't set themselves. And they don't maintain themselves, either. Setting and maintaining boundaries is hard work! In fact, it's so hard that sometimes we're tempted to give up when we're almost there ... just three feet from the gold.

What do you do when you can't quite convince someone to respect your healthy personal boundaries – when all the logic in the world is useless? Do you resign yourself to being disrespected, or do you take a step back and come up with a strategy? What do you when someone gives lip service to your boundaries, ignoring them as soon as they become inconvenient?

If you find it difficult to make your boundaries stick, go back to the chapter on persistence. Think about how you're going to transform your wants and needs from a series of requests, which can be easily ignored, to boundaries with teeth. Will you make it difficult for others to continue their bad behavior – or will you walk away entirely? Or maybe you'll realize that you don't have the power to get what you want right now. Challenges often push us to reconsider our needs. What is your boundary protecting? If it's not connected to one of your highest values, maybe it's OK to let it go. If it is important, then you may need to consider a longer-term approach. What inner and outer resources do you need to protect those values? How will you go about obtaining them? As you can see, resistance isn't the end at all; it's just the beginning.

Overcoming the Obstacles

Do you remember Kyra? She's the one who was so tired of being a doormat. She told her friends that she needed the morning to herself, but it seems they couldn't survive on their own for a few hours. Let's see how she might apply our principles to create a little more balance in her life.

Kyra has a fundamental problem with her beliefs and expectations. She expects her friends to share her values and respect her boundary once she's expressed it. She also treats their needs as more important than her own, buying into the idea that they can't manage without her. They know that her mornings are important to her, but they call anyway. And she's too "polite" to refuse to talk to them.

Kyra also seems to fear confrontation. Rather than stand her ground, she allows herself to be pulled into her friends' dramas. She justifies this by telling herself that there's nothing she can do to change things.

Of course, that's not true. Kyra likes feeling needed – just on her own terms. She was hoping that her friends would postpone their dramas until after lunch. Deep down, she knows that if she's not there, her friends will manage. The crises they come to her with are hardly life-threatening. Without someone like her, Kyra's friends would learn to look after themselves.

Kyra's afraid that if no one needs her, she'll be left alone. She doesn't trust that others will like her for who she is rather than what she does for them. She's trying to buy their friendship by keeping them dependent on her.

But if Kyra wants balance in her life, she'll need to overcome her need to be needed – at least for the morning. If Kyra wasn't so attached to being depended on, she would ignore their calls until she was ready. There would be no crises to deal with until she finished her morning's activities. Yes, they might be unhappy at first. But they'd adjust. And they'd probably still depend on her, although not as much.

And what about Joe, our "regular guy" who must choose between integrity and feeling like one of the boys? What's happening with him?

Joe has a serious inner conflict – one he must resolve by the time he gets to his boss' office. But he's been in conflict ever since Mark started taking long lunches and losing focus. Rather than confronting him, he took on the extra work himself. He saw the extra work as the price he paid for Friday nights with the boys. The sacrifice seemed worthwhile, even though he resented Joe for taking advantage of him.

The problem is that Joe only considered part of the sacrifice. He decided to trade some extra time and effort for being a part of the group. He didn't account for the resentment growing within him, and he certainly didn't think about lying to the boss. The sacrifice turned out to be a lot greater than he expected.

If he had paid more attention to this problem from the beginning, Joe might have realized that the situation wasn't sustainable. Instead of covering for Mark, he could have let him know that their deadlines were intense – and that the boss wouldn't keep anyone around who wasn't pulling his weight. Now his only choices are to lie to the boss (and continue doing Mark's work) or tell the truth and risk losing his place in the Friday night poker game. His decision will depend on how much he wants to belong, how strongly he feels about lying and how much he dislikes taking on someone else's work.

And then there's Laura, who's spent years trying to please controlling and even abusive men. Her friends would beg her to leave, but she always refused. She stayed with every one of those men until they left her for someone else.

Because Laura doesn't feel good about herself, she craves the attention and approval of a man – so much so that she believes she can't live without one. She's a sucker for the dinners, flowers and compliments because they tell her she's OK. Her self-judgment and doubt fades into the background for a while.

Laura relies on her looks and "flexibility" to attract and keep a man. From the moment she recognizes a potential mate, she focuses all her efforts on what she thinks he wants. This is, of course, how she attracts such self-centered men in the first place. And when things turn ugly, she refuses to face the truth. "If I just try a little harder," she tells herself, "I'll get it right this time."

As long as Laura continues to run from her pain, she will attract men who take advantage of her weakness. To move beyond this pattern, she must face her fear of being alone – as well as her deep feelings of unworthiness. It's a goal worth pursuing.

Whether you struggle with intense self-esteem issues like Laura or occasionally "forget" to set the right boundaries, the keys are the same:

1. Know and believe in yourself.
2. See what's really going on.
3. Stop running away from emotional pain and relying on others to make you feel better.
4. Choose boundaries that support your highest values and set them clearly.
5. Maintain those boundaries, even when others make it difficult.

I hope the insights in this book make it possible for you to do just that. Following these simple principles consistently will lead you to a rich and fulfilling life. And isn't that what it's all about?

ABOUT THE AUTHOR

Steph Sterner has spent her life challenging the status quo. As a writer, speaker and teacher, she encourages us to be true to ourselves – to live according to our highest values. This means asking the important questions: What do we believe? Do those beliefs still work for us? What do we value most? And how to do we protect what we value?

Relationships, human nature and emotions are her passion. Through years of study, research, and contemplation – and of course her work with clients and students – she's become an expert in what makes us human.

Steph has a gift for seeing beneath the surface, recognizing the patterns we engage in every day. As a writer, she reveals these sometimes-confusing patterns in simple terms that we can all understand. Rather than give you systems or formulas to follow, she prefers to share universal principles – and lots of examples to help you to apply them for yourself.

Born in the US, Steph now lives in Johannesburg, South Africa – but her search for the meaning and nature of life has taken her from the shamans of Peru to the ashrams of India. When she's not exploring spiritual mysteries, she enjoys hiking and gardening – and just relaxing in the South African sunshine.

www.stephsterner.com

Made in the USA
Lexington, KY
30 January 2019